Urban and Community Development in Atlantic Canada
1867–1991

By The Carleton University
History Collaborative

History Division
Mercury Series Paper 44

Canadian Museum of Civilization

CANADIAN CATALOGUING IN PUBLICATION DATA

Carleton University. History Collaborative

Urban and community development in Atlantic Canada, 1867–1991

(Mercury series, ISSN 0316-1854)
(History; 44)
ISBN 0-660-14017-9

1. Community development, Urban – Atlantic Provinces – History. 2. Urbanization – Atlantic Provinces – History. 3. Atlantic Provinces – Social conditions – History. 4. Atlantic Provinces – Economic conditions – History. I. Canadian Museum of Civilization. II. Title. III. Series. IV. Series: Paper (Canadian Museum of Civilization. History Division); no. 44

HN110.C37 1993   307. 1'416'09715   C93-099660-7

Published by
Canadian Museum of Civilization
100 Laurier Street
P.O. Box 3100, Station B
Hull, Quebec
J8X 4H2

PUBLICATIONS ADVISOR: Peter E. Rider, Atlantic Provinces Historian

COVER PHOTO: William McKee, reproduced by permission of the photographer

MAPS I.2, I.3, I.4, I.5, I.7, I.8, I.9, I.10, III.2, AND IV.2 ARE REPRODUCED FROM: *The Canadian Encyclopedia* by permission of McClelland & Stewart Inc.

COVER DESIGN: Purich Design Studio

HEAD OF PRODUCTION: Deborah Brownrigg

PRODUCTION OFFICER: Lise Rochefort

OBJECT OF THE MERCURY SERIES

The Mercury Series is designed to permit the rapid dissemination of information pertaining to the disciplines in which the Canadian Museum of Civilization is active. Considered an important reference by the scientific community, the Mercury Series comprises over three hundred specialized publications on Canada's history and prehistory.

Because of its specialized audience, the series consists largely of monographs published in the language of the author.

In the interest of making information available quickly, normal production procedures have been abbreviated. As a result, grammatical and typographical errors may occur. Your indulgence is requested.

Titles in the Mercury Series can be obtained by writing to:

Mail Order Services
Publishing Division
Canadian Museum of Civilization
100 Laurier Street
P.O. Box 3100, Station B
Hull, Quebec
J8X 4H2

BUT DE LA COLLECTION MERCURE

La collection Mercure vise à diffuser rapidement le résultat de travaux dans les disciplines qui relèvent des sphères d'activités du Musée canadien des civilisations. Considérée comme un apport important dans la communauté scientifique, la collection Mercure présente plus de trois cents publications spécialisées portant sur l'héritage canadien préhistorique et historique.

Comme la collection s'adresse à un public spécialisé, celle-ci est constituée essentiellement de monographies publiées dans la langue des auteurs.

Pour assurer la prompte distribution des exemplaires imprimés, les étapes de l'édition ont été abrégées. En conséquence, certaines coquilles ou fautes de grammaire peuvent subsister : c'est pourquoi nous réclamons votre indulgence.

Vous pouvez vous procurer la liste des titres parus dans la collection Mercure en écrivant au :

Service des commandes postales
Division de l'édition
Musée canadien des civilisations
100, rue Laurier
C.P. 3100, succursale B
Hull (Québec)
J8X 4H2

ABSTRACT

The pace and scope of urbanization in Atlantic Canada has varied enormously over the past 125 years, giving the region its distinctive urban structure. The region's rural-based economies, much like those in the rest of the country, have proved unable to absorb natural population increases. Towns and cities have only partially accommodated this excess rural population, leading to periods of heavy out-migration.

This book, which arose from a graduate seminar in Maritime history at Carleton University in 1991–92, offers the first systematic and comparative overview of community development for the entire Atlantic region. We initially set out to describe the process of population change against the backdrop of regional political and economic history, but quickly discovered the need to categorize the experience of various communities in order to make sense of the numbers.

The focus of the book is a study of population that assesses the published census returns from Confederation to the present, with the aim of tracking the growth and development of each town and city in the region. The result is a classification in terms of social and economic orientation as well as urban function.

Concentrating on urban growth and decline from a cross-regional perspective offers a framework for understanding the evolution of urban communities. Further analysis, by scholars and community planners alike, can build upon the comparative framework established here.

We also survey aspects of the region's political economy since Confederation, paying close attention to the rise and fall of an industrial core and the emergent dependencies that were being reshaped by the expanding role of government in determining the fate of Atlantic Canadians. A typology of community experiences is followed by a reflection on the consequences for the contemporary urban scene of political and economic transformation.

RÉSUMÉ

Le rythme et l'étendue de l'urbanisation dans la région de l'Atlantique du Canada ont énormément varié au cours des 125 dernières années, façonnant de manière particulière la structure urbaine de cette région. L'économie agricole de la région, du même genre que celle du reste du pays, s'est avérée incapable d'absorber l'accroissement naturel de la population. Les villes, petites et grandes, ont pu accueillir en partie seulement l'excédent de population rurale, d'où des périodes d'exode massif.

Cet ouvrage tire son origine d'un séminaire d'études supérieures, portant sur l'histoire des Maritimes, qui s'est donné à l'université Carleton en 1991-1992. Il constitue le premier aperçu systématique et comparatif du développement collectif de toute la région atlantique. Notre première intention était de décrire le processus du changement démographique avec, en toile de fond, l'histoire politico-économique régionale, mais nous avons vite constaté la nécessité de catégoriser l'expérience de diverses communautés pour que les chiffres parlent.

Le livre consiste en une étude démographique qui interprète les recensements de 1867 à nos jours dans le but de retracer la croissance et le développement de chaque ville de la région. Il en résulte une classification sur le plan de l'orientation socio-économique aussi bien que sur celui de la fonction urbaine.

Le fait de se concentrer sur la croissance et le déclin des villes d'un point de vue interrégional a permis d'établir un schéma pour comprendre l'évolution des collectivités urbaines. Universitaires et urbanistes pourront, à partir du cadre comparatif établi ici, se livrer à une analyse plus poussée.

Nous avons également étudié les aspects de l'économie politique régionale, depuis la Confédération, en nous attardant surtout à la formation et au déclin d'un noyau industriel ainsi qu'aux nouvelles dépendances engendrées par le rôle de plus en plus marqué qu'a joué l'État dans la destinée des Canadiens de l'Atlantique. Une réflexion sur les conséquences des changements politiques et économiques sur le tissu urbain contemporain suit une typologie des expériences collectives.

Table of Contents

List of Figures   4

List of Maps   5

List of Photographs   6

Preface   7

Chapter I
Introduction:
Atlantic Canada's Contemporary Urban System   11

Chapter II
Growth and Decline in Atlantic Canada's Towns and Cities   25

Chapter III
Farm and Fishing Villages:
Zones of Persistent Rurality   51

Chapter IV
Metropolitan and Industrial Zones   75

Chapter V
Conclusion   101

Appendix
Populations of Towns and Cities of Atlantic Canada,
1871–1991   106

Bibliography   119

Contributors   141

Index   143

4

List of Figures

Chapter I
I.1   Population change in the Atlantic Provinces, 1871–1991   *13*
I.2   Population change in the four demographic zones, 1871–1991   *14*

Chapter II
II.1   Urban population rate in Maritimes and Canada, 1871–1911   *31*
II.2   Loss of manufacturing jobs in selected towns, 1912–31   *38*
II.3   Urban population rate in Canada and Atlantic provinces, 1921–91   *41*

Chapter III
III.1   Urban/rural population change in New Brunswick farming areas,   *56*
           1871–1991
III.2   Urban/rural population change in Nova Scotia and Prince Edward   *57*
           Island farming areas, 1871–1991
III.3   Population growth of south shore towns, 1871–1991   *62*
III.4   Urban/rural population change in Nova Scotia littoral zone,   *64*
           1871–1991
III.5   Urban/rural population change in New Brunswick littoral zone,   *66*
           1871–1991
III.6   Population change of northern New Brunswick towns, 1901–91   *68*
III.7   Urban/rural population change in Newfoundland littoral zone,   *71*
           1874–1991

Chapter IV
IV.1   Population growth of metropolitan areas, 1871–1991   *76*
IV.2   Urban/rural population change in Halifax County, 1871–1991   *78*
IV.3   Sectors of employment in Halifax, 1951–86   81
IV.4   Urban/rural population change in Saint John County,   *84*
           1871–1991
IV.5   Sectors of employment in Saint John, 1951–86   *85*
IV.6   Urban/rural population change in Avalon Peninsula, 1874–1991   *86*
IV.7   Sectors of employment in St. John's, 1951–86   *87*
IV.8   Urban/rural population change in Westmorland/Albert and   *91*
           Cumberland Counties, 1871–1991
IV.9   Urban/rural population change in Cape Breton County,   *94*
           1871–1991
IV.10   Urban/rural population change in Pictou County, 1871–1991   *96*
IV.11   Urban/rural population change in Central-Humber,   *98*
           Newfoundland, 1921–91
IV.12   Population change in selected towns, 1951–91   *100*

List of Maps

Chapter I
I.1   Demographic zones of Atlantic Canada   *12*
I.2   Contemporary New Brunswick   *15*
I.3   Metropolitan Saint John   *16*
I.4   Moncton Urban Area   *17*
I.5   Contemporary Nova Scotia   *18*
I.6   Industrial Cape Breton   *19*
I.7   Contemporary Prince Edward Island   *20*
I.8   Charlottetown and Environs   *21*
I.9   Contemporary Newfoundland and Labrador   *23*
I.10   St. John's Urban Area   *24*

Chapter II
II.1   The Maritime railways in 1914[*]   *30*

Chapter III
III.1   Agricultural zones   *53*
III.2   Fredericton Urban Area   *55*
III.3   Littoral zones in Atlantic Canada   *59*

Chapter IV
IV.1   Metropolitan and industrial zones   *76*
IV.2   Halifax and Dartmouth Urban Area   *81*

[*]   Map II.1 courtesy of Shirley Woods *Cinders and Salt Water: A Story of Atlantic Canada's Railways* Halifax, Nimbus, 1992.

6

List of Photographs

Chapter II
Shingle Mill, Sheet Harbour, Nova Scotia   *27*
Cumberland Hotel, Amherst   *29*
Digby waterfront, ca 1910   *33*
Dominion Coal Company, Collier No. 2, Glace Bay, ca 1920   *34*
Downtown Moncton, ca 1920   *36*
Fort Needam Park temporary wartime housing, Halifax, 1943   *39*
Gulf Oil refinery, Port Hawkesbury, ca 1975   *43*
Heavy water plant at Glace Bay, 1971   *48*

Chapter III
Saint Stephen/Milltown, ca 1910   *54*
Mabou coal mines, ca 1905   *61*
Lunenburg boat building, ca 1910   *62*
Yarmouth Post Office, ca 1900   *63*
Chatham, 1910   *65*
Belledune, New Brunswick, 1980   *67*
Two ways of processing fish   *70*
Michelin tire plant, Bridgewater, Nova Scotia   *72*

Chapter IV
The Hydrostone subdivision, Halifax, 1930   *79*
The Halifax waterfront, 1978   *80*
Saint John waterfront, ca 1910   *83*
Scotia Steel blast furnace, Sydney Mines 1903   *89*
Parade at Senator's Corner, Glace Bay, ca 1910   *93*

Preface

Population dynamics and community transformation have proved vexatious questions for scholars of the Atlantic provinces. While regional demographic behaviour has shown interesting departures over the past 125 years, there has been an amazing degree of consistency within some areas and remarkable changes in others. In the twentieth century the region's rural-based economies, much like those in the rest of the country, have proved unable to absorb their natural population increases. Consequently, while rural populations have remained relatively stable over the past 125 years, towns and cities have been unable, except for the period between 1880 and World War I, to accommodate this excess population.

Concentrating our scholarly effort on the net out-flows of people from the region has camouflaged important and ongoing redistributions of the regional population. This book offers the first systematic, comparative overview of community development. It arose from an honours/graduate seminar in Maritime history held at Carleton University during 1991–92. There we set out to describe the process of population change against the backdrop of regional political and economic history. The seminar tracked urban and rural components of the populations of Nova Scotia, New Brunswick, Prince Edward Island and Newfoundland & Labrador from Confederation to the present.

In focusing on urban growth and decline vis a vis neighbouring rural communities from a cross-regional perspective, we pay less attention to the central themes of contemporary urban studies, including the process of town building, which had been so central to community transformation between 1880 and 1920. Even less attention is paid to structural and behavioral aspects of town and city management, or local politics, factors critical to understanding dimensions of class formation for instance. Instead, we offer a framework within which further analysis of these very important aspects of a new social history might be approached by regional scholars and community planners alike.

Rather than offer any dramatic new explanation of the regional experience, we evolved a method for situating the varied experience of urbanization in the context of community development. Analysis of the data yielded a rough typology of rural and urban communities across the region, which forms the basis of the assessments in the following manuscript. Assigning urban and rural qualities to populations within census districts can be problematic at the best of times, but is particularly so prior to 1900. Census tables organized to accommodate the various redistributions of seats in the House of Commons, rather than to accurately reflect demographic relationships within distinct communities, presents problems for analysis. As well, shifting municipal boundaries and the recent trend to create larger metropolitan districts sometimes makes comparative statements perplexing. For analytical purposes, we combined what we felt were similarly oriented census districts from a social and economic perspective to provide a coherent series of four types to reflect different demographic experiences. The four include *Metropolitan Centres, Industrial Centred Towns, Farming Districts and Coastal Littorals*.

Our definition of urban applied a formula of size and density; at least one thousand people, combined with a density of more than 200 persons per square kilometre formed our base requirement for urban designation. This is a more inclusive definition than is common-place, but we did our best to separate which populations in any census district were urban from those which were rural. (The Appendix lists our best estimate of the population of all towns in the region for each census year from 1871 to the present.)

Our work benefitted enormously from the interest and advice of friends and colleagues, who took time to read and discuss all or part of the manuscript with us as it developed. Carman Bickerton, Ron Crawley, Jim Kenny, Bob MacIntosh, Michael Piva, and John Taylor read an early draft and shared their responses with us at Carleton. Rosemary Ommer and Rusty Bitterman offered written critiques. Peter Rider of the Canadian Museum of Civilization read a more developed draft and offered invaluable advice through the process of preparing the manuscript for publication. Special thanks to Bruce Winer of Carleton's Micro-Response Centre for help with the maps.

We offer heart-felt thanks as well to the *Association of Canadian Studies*, whose financial support through their Aid to Publications Program, helped us develop the manuscript for publication. Needless to say, the views expressed are those of the authors rather than of our critics, who might have written a much different book.

Chapter I introduces the region's contemporary urban systems. Chapter II surveys aspects of the political economy of the region since

Confederation, where we pay close attention to the rise and fall of an industrial core and emergence of sets of dependencies reshaped by government's expanding role in determining the fate of Atlantic Canadians. The periodization enunciated in Chapter II provides a context for discussion of various communities taken up in Chapters III and IV, where our typology of community experiences is enunciated. Chapter V offers some reflections on the consequences of the process of transformation for the contemporary urban scene.

D.A. Muise
The Carleton University History Collaborative

Chapter I

Introduction: Atlantic Canada's Contemporary Urban System

Four demographic zones evolved in Atlantic Canada over the past century. They are distinguished by their levels of urban concentration and the functions performed by their towns and cities. Together, these three census metropolitan areas house over a quarter of Atlantic Canadians.[1] Atop the urban hierarchy are the three *Metropolitan Centres* of Halifax, Saint John and St. John's. Between 75% and 90% of residents of their census divisions live within the urban cores. Each, at regional or sub-regional levels dominates a hinterland of its own, though Halifax increasingly is taking on the attributes of the premier regional centre. Fredericton and Charlottetown share some characteristics of metropolitan areas, as there is a considerable amount of similarity in the functions they perform as provincial capitals. But the scale of their activities is so much smaller than that of the metropolitan centres they are not included here.

Industrial Zones are centred on census districts containing Moncton, Sydney and Pictou, and Grand Falls/Corner Brook. In these zones manufacturing, coal mining and other types of resource processing has concentrated large numbers of people in towns which, though they lack the diversity and services available in metropolitan communities, are nonetheless heavily urbanized. Between 50% and 75% of people in these census districts live in towns or cities. While a number of towns outside these industrial zones also developed manufacturing sites at the same time as Sydney, New Glasgow, Amherst, or Moncton, the more limited encounters with industrialization in such towns as Yarmouth and Saint Stephen, for example, had a less decisive impact

---

1. For a discussion of the definition of census metropolitan areas see Richard Nadwodny, *The CMA-CA Program: A Review, 1941–1991* (unpublished Census Canada report, August, 1991).

on their relationship with the surrounding communities. The three Maritime industrial zones took shape between 1880 and 1920, after which their towns and cities generally failed to grow. A number of other towns have grown rapidly since World War II, as a result of new resource processing developments. Newfoundland's single industrial zone is concentrated in two census districts in the central interior of the province, a direct consequence of the emergence there of a pulp and paper industry in Grand Falls and Corner Brook after 1920.[2]

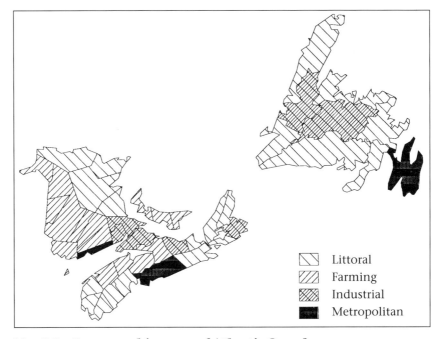

Littoral
Farming
Industrial
Metropolitan

Map I.1   Demographic zones of Atlantic Canada

Much less urbanized are the region's three major *Agricultural Zones:* Nova Scotia's Annapolis Valley, New Brunswick's Saint John Valley and Prince Edward Island. About a third of residents in these three areas live in towns and cities, almost all of which were well established in the pre-industrial era and were spaced to serve the limited functions required by their farming hinterlands. Though there have been dramatic changes in recent years, farming districts generally have

2.   Included for our purposes in Newfoundland's industrial zone is the region's largest census district by size, Labrador. Because of the growth of transport and mining communities there since World War II, its population has assumed a remarkably urban character. Included, also somewhat anomalously, in the Cumberland/Westmorland district is Albert County. Half of Albert county's residents live within the Moncton suburb of Riverview Heights, just across the river from the down-town.

maintained stable urban/rural population ratios over the past century. Most towns in the agricultural districts tend to be quite small, though Truro, Windsor and Saint Stephen have, over the years, hosted textile mills and other types of consumer-oriented or resource processing factories and there are a number of sizable towns. Fredericton and Charlottetown, where there has also been some concentration of service-type industries as well as their functions as provincial capitals, are the two most important cities in these zones.

Towns along *Coastal Littorals* have been mainly gathering points for fish and timber resources. These coastal littorals – most of southern and eastern Nova Scotia, including much of Cape Breton Island, northern New Brunswick and most of Newfoundland – have even more thinly scattered populations than farming areas. Over-all, less than a quarter of their populations live in urban areas and urban/rural ratios have been very stable over the century following Confederation. Changes resulting from government actions and important technological advances in resource processing have occurred since World War II. But in many cases the relationship between these new jobs and urban development has been less directly felt than in previous periods.

Figure I.1   Population change in the Atlantic Provinces, 1871–1991

(Thousands of persons)

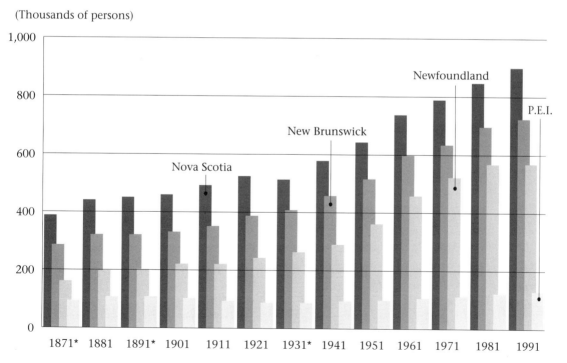

* Newfoundland figures are for 1874, 1894 and 1934.

Overall, the total population of the four Atlantic provinces has increased just 150% during the past one hundred and twenty years, from just under a million in 1871 to almost two and a half million today. Up to 1931, populations within all four provinces had been remarkably stable. Since that time, while Prince Edward Island's population has remained virtually stable, the other three have doubled. Since World War II Newfoundland has experienced the most rapid advance, though that increase may be partially illusory as a consequence of more efficient counting by the federal government, which took responsibility for counting Newfoundlanders after 1949. While Nova Scotia and New Brunswick registered more modest increases, remarkable shifts of their people from one part of their provinces to others occurred.

Within the four demographic zones populations have fluctuated somewhat over time. As one might expect, over time more heavily urbanized areas have appropriated a greater portion of the population. Today approximately a quarter of Atlantic Canadians live in the census divisions of the three metropolitan zones, where once only 10% lived. About 22% live in the four industrial zones. These industrial zones grew rapidly between 1880 and 1920 but have remained relatively stable since that time. 20% live along the coastal littorals, and about 23% in the three agriculturally centred areas. These farming and

Figure I.2   Population change in the four demographic zones, 1871–1991

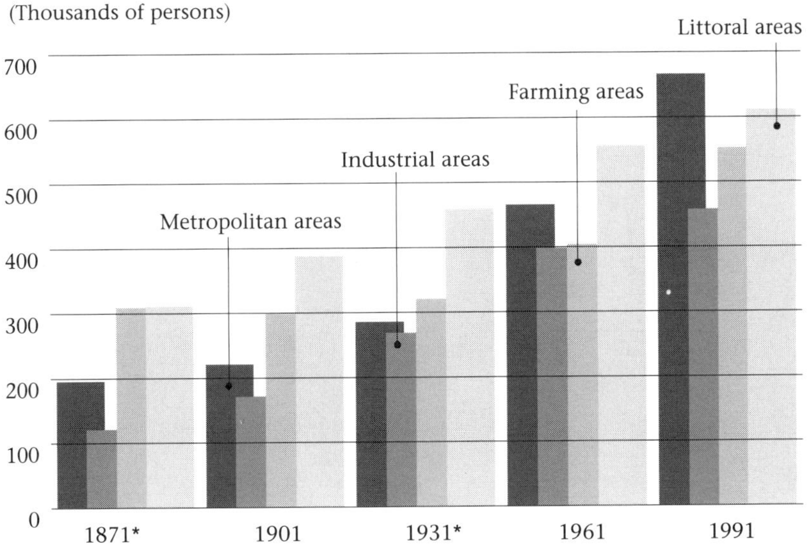

(Thousands of persons)

* Newfoundland figures are for 1874 and 1934.

coastal littoral areas have gradually lost populations since the turn of the century.

Real distinctions between what is urban and what is rural today are problematic at best. These ratios, while reflecting population dynamics within and among census divisions, should be revised to accommodate people who today, in their day to day lives, are increasingly dominated by services and activities available only in towns. Though technically living outside the census boundaries of metropolitan centres or incorporated towns, they have access to most aspects of urban services and cultures with comparative ease.

The Contemporary Urban System

New Brunswick's five cities are close to the province's four corners and near its centre.[3] Straddling the mouth of the Saint John River near the province's south-west corner, the city of Saint John has the province's largest concentration of urban residents. Metropolitan Saint John today stretches east, west and north to incorporate a number of suburban areas that include virtually the entire population of Saint John

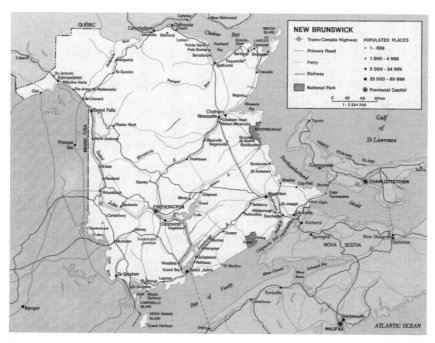

Map I.2   Contemporary New Brunswick

3.   All population figures in this section are from: Statistics Canada, *Urban Areas: Population and Dwelling Counts, 1991* (Ottawa, 1992), Table 4.

County. North and east, areas in neighbouring Kings County have been effectively integrated into the greater Saint John area as well.[4]

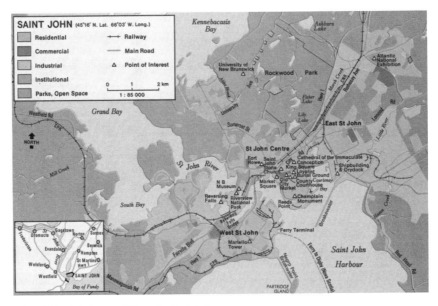

Map I.3   Metropolitan Saint John

Moncton, the province's second largest city, emerged as an industrial, service and distribution centre following establishment of the Intercolonial Railroad's eastern headquarters there in 1876. Since World War I it has become an urban centre for New Brunswick's many Acadians, serving as the headquarters for various insurance and benevolent societies as well as an educational centre following expansion of the campus of the Université de Moncton. Its heavily bilingual population has attracted regional offices of many federal agencies, making it an administrative centre for the delivery of many government programs throughout the region. This adaptability has permitted it to continue growing despite virtual disappearance of its traditional economic activities, such as the Canadian National Railway shops and the regional distribution centre for the T. Eaton Company (see Map I.4).

Fredericton, about mid-way up the St. John River, blossomed as a service centre for a robust agricultural area bordering the river valley. Though it does not compete with Saint John for provincial economic leadership, its stature as the provincial capital gives it a certain precedence within the province's urban system. In recent years expanded

4.   David Boucher, "Metropolitan Growth in Atlantic Canada: The Saint John Throughway," M.A. Thesis (Canadian Studies),Carleton University, 1993.

government and educational functions have swollen its population, so that now its metropolitan area stretches north and south along both sides of the river, as well as eastward along the Nashwaak River, which empties into the Saint John River across from Fredericton. It's metropolitan grasp extends south to absorb the satellite town of Oromocto, near the province's largest military establishment at Canadian Forces Base Gagetown just a few miles down-river.

Only since World War I have urban centres emerged in New Brunswick's northern corners. Villages established there earlier in the nineteenth century as gathering and processing centres for the lumber industry have become regional centres. The pulp and paper based towns of Campbellton, Bathurst and Dalhousie, located along the south side of the Bay of Chaleurs, have surpassed older lumber towns such as Chatham and Newcastle, established earlier in the nineteenth century near the mouth of the Miramichi River. Edmundston, close to both the Quebec and American borders at the province's northwest corner, serves predominantly francophone Madawaska County, its economy dominated by the massive pulp and paper mill established there in the 1920s.

Both these northern zones in fact continue to be dominated by externally controlled pulp and paper manufacturers and new base-metals companies, who take advantage of the large labour surpluses and diverse timber and mineral reserves of the northern areas. In effect, as "resource enclaves", they remain dependent on distant

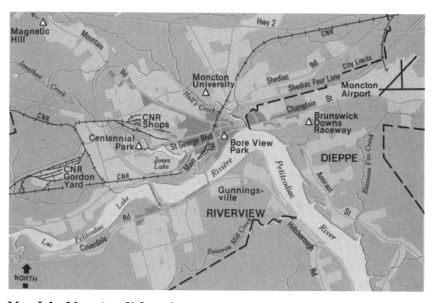

Map I.4   Moncton Urban Area

capitalists who control the harvesting, processing and marketing of
their staples, a condition stretching back to the nineteenth century.
Recently, these staples gathering and processing activities have been
supplanted by the commercial and administrative functions needed to
deliver a wide range of government services to their expanding populations. Economically driven or government based programs for development designed to attract new industries to the district have had led
to dramatic improvements to social and educational services, especially in such areas as roads and port facilities, etc., much of it to
accommodate base metals industries established in Gloucester County
and the expanded the capacity of the fishing industry of the "Acadian
Peninsula".

Nova Scotia
With nearly half of Nova Scotia's population and over two thirds of
all its urban dwellers, Halifax and Cape Breton counties dominate the
urban life of the province. Over the past two decades metro Halifax
has been the fastest growing community in the entire region, even
though, like the other two metro centres of the region, the city proper
ceased growing several decades ago. While Halifax's political primacy
over the rest of the province was assured the moment it was named
capital in 1749, it achieved only tenuous economic influence over a

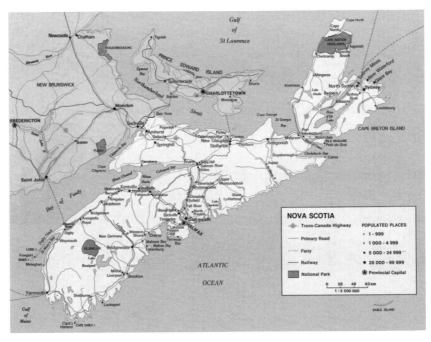

Map I.5   Contemporary Nova Scotia

diverse colony through the nineteenth century. Yet it developed a political and bureaucratic infrastructure necessary for governing the large province and has had the largest military establishment since its foundation.

Dartmouth, facing Halifax across the harbour, is Nova Scotia's second largest city and a dynamic and expansive community in its own right. Beyond Bedford Basin lie the bedroom towns of Bedford and Lower Sackville. In fact, growth of in these suburbs accounts for virtually all of the province's population increase between 1986 and 1991, just 28,000. The metro area also has the region's most transient population, with large numbers of young workers and post-secondary students thronging into its service industries and educational institutions on a continuous and apparently revolving basis. As well, mainland Nova Scotians from as far away as Truro, Windsor and Lunenburg are increasingly drawn into its sphere of influence for services and entertainment.

Like so many resource based cities, Sydney owes its position to a natural harbour, in its case centring on the region's richest coal field. During Cape Breton Island's glorious independence from 1784 to 1820 Sydney had been capital of the struggling colony. But through most of the nineteenth century it was little more than a small service community of less than 1,500 residents. Organization of a major steel plant there in 1900, and the dramatic expansion of several nearby coal mining towns between 1890 and 1910, turned it into a major industrial

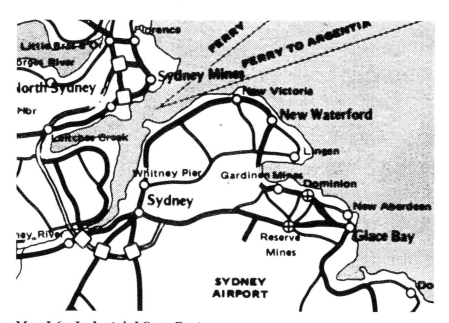

Map I.6   Industrial Cape Breton

and commercial city. Though the city's population still does not exceed 30,000, the broader metro area holds closer to 120,000, 70% of all Cape Bretoners. Since 1956 the mainland has been connected to Cape Breton by a causeway. This has focused a certain amount of the metropolitan function off-Island, particularly as improvements to transportation have eased access to Halifax for residents of the area.

No other town in Nova Scotia has exceeded 10,000 in population and most stabilized in the 1920s, after a relatively short period of economic growth. The urban complex surrounding New Glasgow holds just under 30,000 in its five coal-mining and metals fabricating towns, where the industrial base has recently been supplemented by a major pulp mill and one of the three Michelin tire manufacturing plants built in Nova Scotia after the 1960s.

Truro, near the physical centre of the province, became a significant transportation and industrial town prior to 1920 and serves as well as an educational and agricultural service centre. Amherst, Springhill, Yarmouth and Bridgewater have all experienced periods of industrial activity that produced population booms of some proportions, but most of the industries in these towns have long since vanished. All continue to perform local metropolitan functions at a subregional level, but none has developed much of an urban complex. In recent years many of them have developed their service industries, assisted by development of a provincial highway system that provides

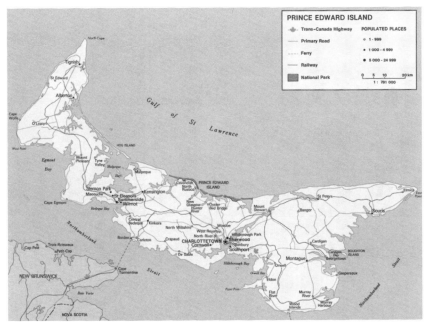

Map I.7   Contemporary Prince Edward Island

easy access to their burgeoning strip malls and shopping centres for virtually every rural resident of the province.

Prince Edward Island

Prince Edward Island is barely a few dozen kilometres wide in most places, so almost everyone has access to tide-water. This permitted a profusion of tiny villages to service its mostly rural mixed farming, fishing and lumbering communities during the period of settlement. Mostly because of the absence of any significant waste lands, it has the densest population of any province in the country. As provincial capital, Charlottetown has always enjoyed primacy. But, like the rest of PEI, political and economic development was stymied by the indifference of absentee land-owners until the middle of the nineteenth century. Today Charlottetown's population barely exceeds 15,000, though a complex of suburban communities surrounding the capital raises its metro area population to about 25,000, over a quarter of all Islanders (see Map I.7).

Toward the end of the nineteenth century Summerside emerged as Prince Edward Island's second town, primarily as a service centre for the rich farm and fishing areas of the northern half of the Island. Since World War II, its service role has been enlarged by the establishment of a large air base nearby. Elsewhere villages of a few hundred people continue to support the agricultural and fishing activities of their sub-areas. A fair amount of seasonality characterizes many of these   villages, particularly in the more highly developed tourist areas on the North Shore area, where summer populations can double for a few weeks. Charlottetown's primacy increased with recent improvements to transportation, a domination that is compromised by the ease of access to the mainland, to which many Islanders are drawn for many of their needs.

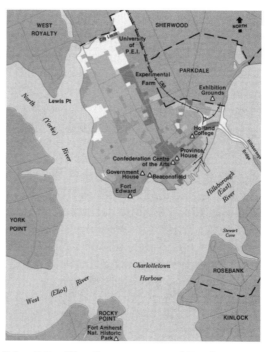

Map I.8   Charlottetown and Environs

Newfoundland

Before it entered Canada in 1949, Newfoundland was largely under-developed from an urban perspective. Yet today, with over 53% of its population living in towns and cities, its urban/rural ratio is second only to Nova Scotia's in the region. As fishing was the only significant economic activity prior to this century, virtually every Newfoundlander lived on or near tide-water, most in tiny outports scattered along its coasts. In fact, since no legislative encouragement was given for municipal incorporation, little urbanization was evident outside St. John's. Recent changes to fishing and fish processing technologies, along with the administrative imperatives associated with the provincial government's delivery of services such as schools and hospitals, has forced consolidation of many of these coastal communities into so-called "designated growth centres" (see Map I.9).

With just under half of the province's population, the Avalon Peninsula, is Newfoundland's most densely populated corner. St. John's, near its eastern tip, has served as capital and principal port since the eighteenth century. Today, one in three Newfoundlanders lives in St. John's metro area. Its merchants still control much of the province's economic development, though a restructured and techno-logically advanced fishing industry, which faces a radical crisis of depletion, interacts with national and international capitalism in ways it seldom did before. Possibilities of off-shore petroleum development offer the potential for even more change in the near future, which St. John's merchants are determined to direct to their benefit.

Only after construction of a trans-island railway in the closing decades of the nineteenth century did significant urban development occur outside the capital. This was tied to emergence of a pulp and paper industry at Grand Falls and Corner Brook. The iron ore deposits on Bell Island, in Conception Bay, and other mineral exploitation at locations across southern Newfoundland had planted small towns in a number of places, all of them tied to off-island demand for their particular resource. The largest of them, the Wabana development on Bell Island, was tied directly into the large coal and steel corporations which dominated industrial Cape Breton.

Corner Brook and Grand Falls, the second and third largest towns outside the metro area, only emerged with development of pulp and paper mills there following World War I. Both communities would require concentrations of workers and services far beyond the exigen-cies of the traditional dried cod fishery, which placed a high premium on keeping available land free for spreading out the cod. Apart from the post-1950s mining, transportation and hydro-electric develop-ments in Labrador, few other urban nodes have developed beyond the status they held prior to Confederation, though a number of fish processing centres have grown substantially since then. Labrador's Wabush/Labrador City and Happy Valley/Goose Bay typify the resource and service towns established across the Canadian north in the post World War II era.

Maps I.9   Contemporary Newfoundland and Labrador

The political economy of modern states has resulted in a complex transportation system linking towns and countrysides for various services and commercial activities. Atlantic Canada's contemporary urban system is increasingly integrated and dependent, reflecting the degree to which municipalities have become clients of provincial governments as well as the degree to which the four provinces have themselves become clients of the federal government. The primacy of Halifax and the other provincial capitals as deliverers of services and as transfer points for federal and other grants is quite remarkable. On the other hand, important areas of the region continue as resource enclaves, most of their economic activity continuing to be directed from elsewhere, with few links to the remainder of the regional economy, a shortcoming that has been reinforced by the sometimes desperate search for capital to overcome the economic doldrums of communities within the region. As more of the region's economic endeavour rests in fewer and fewer hands, economic links between communities weaken.

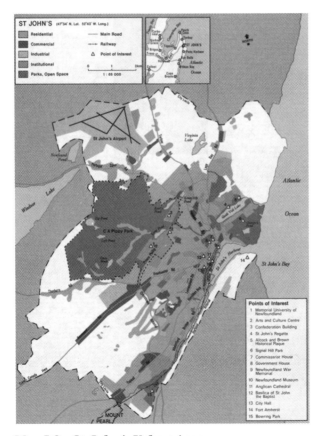

Map I.2   St. John's Urban Area

Chapter II

Growth and Decline in Atlantic Canada's Towns and Cities

Atlantic Canada's urbanization occurred in four distinct but overlapping phases: (1) from Confederation to the closing decade of the nineteenth century, when a regional rail network was integrated with that of central Canada; (2) from the 1890s to World War I, a period when much of the region's secondary industry was established; (3) from the 1920s to the 1940s, when, following collapse of the industrial core and depression of various staples trades, many towns and cities declined in both absolute and relative terms; and (4) from the 1950s to the present, characterized by increased concentration of populations in larger metropolitan centres and a restructuring of local political relationships across the region.

J.M.S. Careless, dean of Canadian urban historians, argues that Canada's cities grew by exerting dominance over expanding resource hinterlands, an approach which tends to marginalize the Atlantic region by stressing its remoteness from the more profitable resource frontiers of North America's interior.[1] This corroborates the work of H.A. Innis and S.A. Saunders, stressing the absence of any need for a dominant metropolitan centre because of the rather unstructured nature of traditional fish and lumbering staples. L.D. McCann uses a similar paradigm to explain Halifax's failure to develop into a regional industrial centre, and extends the analysis to explain lower levels of urbanization in the region during the post-Confederation era.[2]

1. J.M.S. Careless, "Aspects of Metropolitanism in Atlantic Canada," in *Regionalism in the Canadian Community, 1867–1967,* Mason Wade (ed.) (Toronto, 1969); and his *Frontier and Metropolis: Regions, Cities and Identities in Canada before 1914* (Toronto, 1989).
2. L.D. McCann, "Staples and the New Industrialism in the Growth of Post-Confederation Halifax," in *Acadiensis* VIII, 2 (Spring 1979); "'Living the Double Life': Town and Country in the Industrialization of the Maritimes," in *Geographical Perspectives*

Careless's frontier-metropolis approach (heartland-hinterland in McCann's lexicon) depicts urbanization as a function of interaction and linkage between manufacturing and resource exploitation. The question remains as to whether or not highly developed cities were necessary for development to occur or if it was the other way round.

By Careless' calculation, economic and administrative activity can only be concentrated where metropoles are fully integrated with exploiting and processing regional resources through servicing rich hinterlands. Several analyses assert that urban under-development is a prime factor in Atlantic Canada's failure to match general Canadian expectations regarding an acceptable living standard in the twentieth century. A series of ecological and demographic analyses, emphasize the adverse effects of lower income levels and traditions of multiple occupations and weak secondary manufacturing or resource process-ing bases are used to explain underdevelopment. Studying the urban-ization of Atlantic Canada, however, demands that more factors be taken into account, though any analysis must begin with the specific and somewhat uneven experience of development and underdevelop-ment across the region.[3]

Maritimers and Newfoundlanders participated successfully in the North Atlantic staples economies of the nineteenth century, prosper-ing and suffering with demand cycles of distant markets for fish, tim-ber, farm produce and, by mid-century, coal. Ships from the region carried regional staples to the far corners of the Atlantic at least. Arti-sanal activity occurred on a small scale in most of these pre-industrial urban nodes, but much of the processing technology was imported, as were most manufactured goods necessary for producing the staples or carrying on everyday life in the resource producing areas.[4]

on the Maritime Provinces, Douglas Day (ed.) (Halifax, 1988); and Heartland and Hin-terland: A Geography of Canada (Toronto, 1987).

3.   Eric Sager, "Dependency, Underdevelopment, and the Economic History of the Atlantic Provinces," in Acadiensis XVII, 1 (Autumn, 1987); Peter J. Wylie, "When Markets Fail: Electrification and Maritime Industrial Decline in the 1920s," in Aca-diensis XVII, 1 (Autumn 1987); R. Brym and J. Sacouman (eds.), Underdevelopment and Social Movements in Atlantic Canada (Toronto, 1979); and B. Fairley et. al., Restructuring and Resistance: Perspectives from Atlantic Canada (Toronto, 1990). Two suggestive alternatives to this approach are Ian McKay, "The Crisis of Dependent Development: Class Conflict in the Nova Scotia Coalfields, 1872–1876," in Class, Gender, and Region: Essays in Canadian Historical Sociology, Gregory S. Kealey (ed.) (St. John's, 1988); and L. Anders Sandberg, "Dependent Development, Labour and the Trenton Steel Works, Nova Scotia, c.1900–1943," in Labour/Le Travail 27 (Spring, 1991).

4.   Eric Sager and Gerald Panting, Maritime Capital: The Shipping Industry in Atlantic Canada, 1820–1914 (Montreal, 1990); Richard MacKinnon, "Carriage Making in St. John's, Nfld.: A Folkloristic Perspective on a Historical Industry," in Material His-tory Bulletin/Bulletin d'histoire de la culture materielle 27 (Spring, 1988).

Prior to Confederation, apart from Halifax, Saint John and St. John's, few communities exhibited many urban characteristics. Though Fredericton and Charlottetown, by virtue of their political status as colonial capitals, were significantly larger than villages, even they had narrowly restricted urban qualities. Villages seldom held more than five hundred people, and only a few had populations larger than a thousand.[5] Depending on small hinterlands for development, most towns were located at tide-water or on accessible rivers and varied greatly in size and status. Delivery of services and trans-shipment of staples changed somewhat with improvements to transportation and communications at mid-century, particularly in Nova Scotia and New Brunswick, where railways prompted a new economic vision extending beyond the dependence on staples typical of the previous century. Central to that vision was the notion that towns had to become more actively involved in the economic life of the colonies if the population of outlying areas was to be retained. Prince Edward Island and Newfoundland, which only acquired their own railways later in the century, failed to develop these urban preoccupations.[6]

Areas where farming predominated, with their more densely

Shingle Mill, Sheet Harbour, Nova Scotia
Small mills like this one dotted the coasts and rivers of the region, producing a wide variety of products for both regional and export markets. Though they were often operated on a seasonal basis, markets for lumber would be so expansive during the region's industrial development they could hardly keep up with demand. Steam-powered, for the most part by regionally manufactured engines by the turn of the century, they were among the most efficient producers of lumber products anywhere. *Source: Public Archives of Nova Scotia*

5. Most apparently urban-centred census districts were townships rather than towns. Widespread town incorporation, which did not occur until the last decade of the nineteenth century, improves population estimates a great deal after 1900.
6. Rosemary Langhout, "Developing Nova Scotia: Railways and Public Accounts, 1848–1867," in *Acadiensis* XVI, 2 (Spring, 1985); and C.M. Wallace, "Saint John Boosters and the Railroads in Mid-Nineteenth Century," in *Acadiensis* VI, 1 (Autumn, 1976); James Hiller, "The Railway and Local Politics in Newfoundland, 1870–1901," in *Newfoundland in the Nineteenth and Twentieth Centuries: Essays in Interpretation,* James Hiller and Peter Neary (eds.) (Toronto, 1980).

populated surrounding farm lands, demanded higher levels of services than fishing or timber resource based areas. There was, however, always considerable overlap between areas, particularly following development of a more labour and technology intensive sawn lumber industry in the post-1850s era. Timber making had, to some degree, complemented agricultural settlement, at least during the pioneer phase, when off-farm labour provided the necessary credits permitting settlers to gain the manufactured goods needed to improve their lands. Timber towns, much like fishing ports, often acted as little more than trans-shipment points until the sawn-lumber industry demanded much larger infusions of technology and stable work-forces to turn timber into various lumber products. Water or steam powered sawmills also required more investment in stationary equipment, a development with important implications for towns directly affected. Often the livelihood of communities was a function of diverse sets of dependencies that operated when urban and rural areas were inter-twined in all aspects of development.[7]

Confederation to The National Policy

On the eve of Confederation, urban areas held less than 15% of the region's population. By the 1920s, closer to half of Maritimers lived in towns and cities. Demographic relationships between towns and their hinterlands were significantly reshaped by new trends in the political and economic experience of the region. Improvements in transportation and communications created a much more inter-dependent economic and social system, though not always at the same time in all places. Expansion and integration of the region's railway system was the major accomplishment of the immediate post-Confederation period. The limited and unconnected railways created in the 1850s in Nova Scotia and New Brunswick, and in the 1860s and 1870s in Prince Edward Island, were brought together under the new Inter colonial Railroad, whose Moncton-based management took over all these rather disjointed pre-Confederation lines, linked them together and constructed branch lines to many new communities in the region. These links were promoted actively by local capitalists anxious to tap into regional markets.[8]

Between 1876 and World War I, the Inter colonial alone more than doubled its track to almost 5,000 kilometres and extended its

---

7. G. Wynn, *Timber Colony: A Historical Geography of Early Nineteenth Century New Brunswick* (Toronto, 1981); Barbara Robertson, *Sawpower: Making Lumber in the Sawmills of Nova Scotia* (Halifax, 1986).
8. Shirley Woods, *Cinders and Salt Water: The Story of Atlantic Canada's Railways* (Halifax, 1992).

Cumberland Hotel, Amherst
This scene typified pre-industrial main streets. Hotels such as the Cumberland House, commonly served both commercial travellers and temporary residents. Amherst, which would emerge as one of the region's primary industrial centres later in the century, was initially a lumber processing and agricultural supply centre for Cumberland County and the surrounding Tantramar Marshes area that formed Nova Scotia's boundary with New Brunswick. *Source: Cumberland County Historical Society*

lines in Quebec from Riviere du Loup to Montreal.[9] Other railways were also built, including the Canadian Pacific's "Short-Line", completed from Montreal across northern Maine to Saint John in the early 1890s, and the Dominion and Atlantic, which combined a number of shorter lines to connect Halifax to Yarmouth through the Annapolis Valley. Track in the region approached 10,000 kilometres by 1900, excluding the several hundred kilometres laid by the Newfoundland Railroad during the 1880s and 1890s to connect St. John's with the west coast of the Island at Port-Aux-Basques (see Map II.1).

These lines connected towns never before linked by effective overland communication. Low freight rates on the government owned lines were intended to guarantee producers of a wide variety of staples and manufactured products access to regional and central Canadian markets. It also promoted the growth of manufacturing towns along the line. Newfoundland's railway priorities were aimed at diversifying

9.   Ernest R. Forbes, "Misguided Symmetry: The Destruction of Regional Transportation Policy for the Maritimes," in *Canada and the Burden of Unity*, David Jay Bercuson (ed.) (Toronto, 1977); Ken Cruikshank, *Close Ties: Railways, Government, and the Board of Railway Commissioners, 1851–1933* (Montreal/Kingston, 1991)

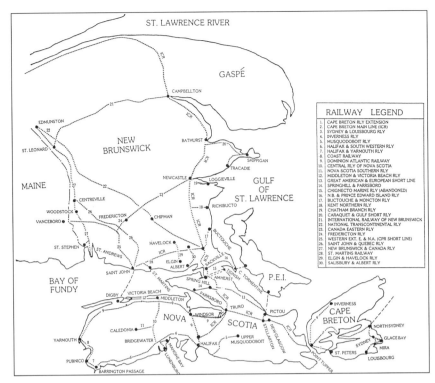

Map II.1   The Maritime railways in 1914

its industrial development to include forestry and mining. Though it plunged the colony into debt, the railway ultimately helped unify its centres of population and increased the scope of its economy.

Controversy regarding the impact of railways on community development and the consequences of subsequent rationalization of routes and freight rates should not cloud our understanding that there was little dispute at the time they were the centre-piece of economic transformation within the region. Though very little of the staples produced in the region depended on the railways for the transport of their products, either within or outside the region.[10]

10. Dean Jobb, "The Politics of the New Brunswick and Prince Edward Railway, 1872–1886," in *Acadiensis* XIII, 2 (Spring 1984): 69; Ken Cruikshank, "The People's Railway: The Intercolonial Railway and the Canadian Public Enterprise Experience," in *Acadiensis* XVI, 1 (Autumn, 1986); Ken Cruikshank, "The Intercolonial Railway, Freight Rates and the Maritime Economy," in *Acadiensis* XXII, 1 (Autumn, 1992); James Hiller, "The Railway and Local Politics in Newfoundland..."; and David Alexander, "Newfoundland's Traditional Economy and Development to 1934," both in *Newfoundland in the Nineteenth and Twentieth Centuries...*; Leo Blaise Doyle, "Politics, Policy Making and the Role of Local Elites: The Amherst Board of Trade and the Formation of Transportation Policy for the Maritimes 1906–1918," M.A. research paper, Carleton University, 1991.

The National Policy Era to World War I

During the National Policy era, even though industrialization attracted people to towns, urban growth remained quite uneven. New Brunswick, which had started with the highest ratio of its population in towns, failed to keep pace with Nova Scotia during the *National Policy* era. Though Nova Scotia's urban proportions never equaled Canadian averages, its urban/rural profile closely paralleled that of Canada as a whole during those years.

Figure II.1 Urban population rate in Maritimes and Canada, 1871–1911

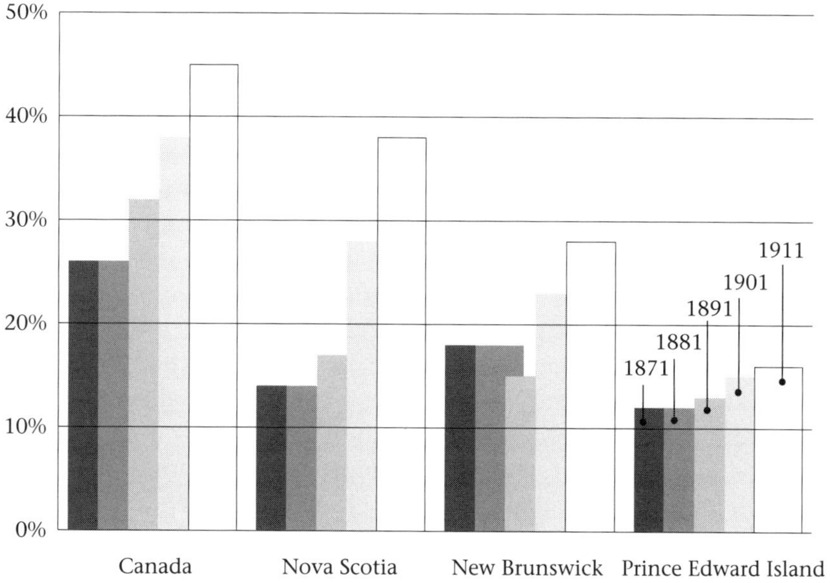

Source: Census Canada estimates (rounded off).

Industrialization and urban development were inter-dependent, so Newfoundland and Prince Edward Island which remained the least industrialized were also least urbanized. Regional entrepreneurs adapted their towns to higher levels of capitalization, using new technologies such as cotton mills and steel plants. As well, a range of consumer oriented industries and new resource processing factories were introduced. Many of the technologies developed in the United States or Great Britain were transferred to the Maritimes with little change.

These industries needed large labour forces at or near the point of production. Towns such as Amherst, Pictou and Sydney drew upon surplus labour from surrounding rural areas, in the process reducing the number of migrants that for so long had headed to New England.

Where this industrial formation flourished, local capital shaped a new urban landscape, a process facilitated by widespread municipal incorporation. Thirty towns were incorporated in the three Maritime provinces between 1880 and 1920, where there had been only five at Confederation.[11]

During this National Policy era, when federal tariffs on manufactured goods and the expansion of railways provided alternate investment opportunities for local entrepreneurs a new pattern of urbanization was entrenched in the region. Local elites, with their activities based on real-estate and commercial development, provided services to burgeoning town populations with an aggressive program of urban transformation. Electricity, running water, telephones, and a number of other innovations, based on coal-powered, steam-based technologies transformed the material conditions of daily life in the region's towns. Across the region, urban infrastructures such as roads, sewers and utilities were developed. Hospitals, churches, schools and various kinds of recreation facilities were built, at enormous public expense, in order to satisfy the needs of larger numbers of workers. This great rush to establish and maintain the appearance of modernity was designed to attract more investment.

Coal and steel towns that depended on external sources of capital seldom developed their urban landscapes and services to levels of those founded on local entrepreneurship. For instance, the Nova Scotia Steel and Coal Company, which took over the mines at Sydney Mines from the General Mining Association in 1900, saw little need to attract capitalists to the town through improved civic conditions. As a result, the community failed to develop either the services or commercial district characteristic of other communities its size. Both Dominion Steel and Coal and Nova Scotia Steel and Coal satisfied their own water and power needs with their own plants, selling their surplus to town residents. Until well into the 1920s, they would also control much of the housing and retail trade throughout industrial Cape Breton and Springhill, and to a lesser extent in New Glasgow, through their ownership of housing and stores.[12]

Through the first two decades of the twentieth century, growth was seen as the key to development. However, outside of coal towns, new capital investment failed to reach many resource-processing

11. T.W. Acheson, "The National Policy and the Industrialization of the Maritimes, 1880–1910," in *Acadiensis* I, 2 (Spring, 1972); L.D. McCann "Staples and the New Industrialism..."; and D.A. Muise, "The Industrial Context of Inequality: Female Participation in Nova Scotia's Paid Labour Force, 1871–1921," in *Acadiensis* XX, 2 (Spring, 1991). See as well, Kris Inwood (ed.), *Farm, Factory and Fortune: New Studies in the Economic History of the Maritime Provinces* (Fredericton, 1983).
12. D.A. Muise, "'The Great Transformation': Changing the Urban Face of Nova Scotia, 1871–1921," in *Nova Scotia Historical Review* XI, 3 (Autumn 1991).

enclaves, where the absence of local economic development continued to provoke out-migration. At the same time, some towns were linked into a web of interdependence that would have been inconceivable a generation earlier. Manufacturers' associations, professional and middle-class reform groups and a number of religious organizations took advantage of better communications to create a more fully integrated regional community. This economic consolidation prompted new levels of "boosterism", as towns competed with one another for industries.[13]

Digby waterfront, ca 1910
While many towns expanded dramatically during the National Policy era, others continued much as they had before. Digby continued its direct dependence on small-scale local merchants. With their stores backed directly onto the docks, they had few requirements for the extensive new transportation systems that were becoming commonplace in more expansive towns. Though even in the case of Digby there were important developments with the arrival of the railroad and its role as a terminus for the Dominion Atlantic Railroad's ferry service to Saint John. *Source: United Church of Canada Archives*

13.   "Boosterism" is defined as a desire to encourage growth, a high degree of community spirit and suspicion of elites in other centres, often combined with a scorn for organized labour and the poor. See. Alan F.J. Artibise, "Patterns of Prairie Urban Development, 1871–1950," in *Eastern and Western Perspectives,* P.A. Buckner and David J. Bercuson (eds.) (Toronto, 1981); and *Prairie Urban Development, 1870–1930* (Ottawa, 1981). On the response of regional elites see E.R. Forbes, *The Maritime Rights Movement, 1919–1927: A Study in Canadian Regionalism* (Montreal/Kingston, 1979). More specific is Leo Doyle *Politics, Policy Making and the Role of Local Elites…;*

As capitalists and urban middle classes redefined the urban milieu within a progressive vision, so too did workers come to redefine their version of what constituted a fair share of the wealth generated through labour. Transiency and rapid population growth during the building phase of the National Policy era had fostered a sense of insecurity for many workers. The period was one of great transformation for the working classes as conflicts over the nature of relations between labour and capitalism and the role of unions in determining the nature of work situations was questioned. The consolidation of Canadian capitalism during World War I prompted a level of class consciousness and unionization, primarily among skilled workers in the industrial zone between Moncton and Sydney, but among the building tradesmen of Halifax and Saint John as well. During periods of high demand for their labour,

Dominion Coal Company Colliery No. 2 Glace Bay, ca 1920
Aside from the steel plants erected at Sydney and Sydney Mines, coal mines were the region's largest industrial establishments. Haulage equipment and storage facilities were the tip of the iceberg, supporting the work of the miners below ground, which spread for several kilometres through a labyrinth of underground workings. These massive surface workings supported as many as a thousand men underground, dominated coal towns; their whistles, signalling events underground, struck the cadence for daily life. *Source: National Archives of Canada*

See as well, Stephen Burridge, "The Busy East, 1910–1925." M.A. Thesis Carleton University, 1993.

coal-miners, acting through their union, the Provincial Workmen's Association, could threaten to halt or slow industrialization, a power coal companies countered by summoning the state to repress strikes, a tactic which was invoked many times.[14]

During World War I workers everywhere turned labour shortages into substantial wage gains, which would subsequently be taken away when the economy declined once again in the 1920s, provoking the most intensive period of labour strife in the region's history. War, by boosting sagging industrial economies across the country, had provided economic relief to industrial communities everywhere. In the Maritimes, it provided the occasion for Canadian, American and British capitalists to complete the consolidation regional the industrial structure with that of the heartland. Outside capital was mobile enough to withdrew investments from the region soon after the war, causing production cutbacks, economic stagnation and job loss. In the aftermath, workers involved themselves more directly in urban politics, where they contributed a great deal.[15]

The Inter-War Years

Following World War I, the demographic pull of industrial towns and cities on their surrounding rural areas declined sharply. Where industrialization had carved durable new urban patterns, economic stagnation now smothered potential for the more fully-integrated regional urban network that had provided the framework for economic advance in the previous decades. The social fabric of debt-ridden towns disintegrated in the wake of industrial collapse. Soon out-migration began to affect towns and cities, much as it had been ravaging the country-side for generations. Political responses such as the Maritime Rights Movement and a new socialist consciousness failed to

14. Literature on the rise of the working class in Nova Scotia is voluminous. Among others, one could consult: Ian Mckay, "Strikes in the Maritimes, 1901–1914," in *Atlantic Canada After Confederation: The Acadiensis Reader Volume Two*, P.A. Buckner and David Frank (eds.) (Fredericton, 1988); David Frank, "Class Conflict in the Coal Industry: Cape Breton, 1922," in *Essays in Canadian Working Class History*, Peter Warrian and Gregory S. Kealey (eds.) (Toronto, 1976); Donald McGillivray, "Military Aid to the Civil Power: The Cape Breton Experience in the 1920s," in *Acadiensis* III,2 (Spring, 1974); Nolan Reilly, "The General Strike in Amherst, Nova Scotia, 1919," in *Acadiensis* IX, 2 (Spring, 1980); Ian McKay, *The Craft Transformed: An Essay on the Carpenters of Halifax, 1885–1985* (Halifax, 1985).

15. L. Anders Sandberg, "Dependent Development, Labour and the Trenton Steel Works..."; David Frank, "Company Town/Labour Town: Local Government in the Cape Breton Coal Towns, 1917–1926," in *Histoire sociale/Social History* XIV, 27 (May, 1981); for Newfoundland see Jessie Chisholm, "Organizing on the Waterfront: The St. John's Longshoremen's Protective Union (LSPU), 1890–1914"; and Peter McInnis, "All Solid on the Line: The Reid Newfoundland Strike of 1918," both in *Labour/Le Travail* 26 (Fall, 1990).

stanch the haemorrhage, which would have worsened in the 1930s if economic migrants had been able to escape the region during the more widespread depression of that decade. But destinations were no longer as inviting as they had been and Maritimer governments had to administer large urban establishments without the incomes and taxation based upon which they had been founded so optimistically only a few years earlier.

Downtown Moncton, ca 1920
The impact of railways on the region was most profoundly felt in Moncton, where it sliced through the centre of town to divided the community into its older more staid commercial functions, close to the waterfront, and the new industrial centre linked to the railway. In the process smokestacks came to rival church spires for dominance of the urban skyline. *Source: United Church of Canada Archives*

Fishing, lumbering and farming communities remained viable, but operated at reduced capacity, while the difficult economic situation inhibited further urbanization. Some rural areas, which had been the source of many of urban workers, were able to re-absorb some unemployed workers and their families from industrial centres undergoing collapse.[16]

16. This down-turn of the regional community has been one of the most actively pursued subjects in recent historical enquiry. It follows the series of enquiries that were undertaken by all levels of government during the 1920s and 1930s. The Duncan Royal Commission (Maritime Claims) (1926), and the Rowell-Sirois Royal Commission (Dominion Provincial Relations) were the most important of these at the federal level, though there were a number of others. K.G. Jones, "Response to Regional Disparity in the Maritime Provinces, 1926–1942: A Study in Intergovernmental

The "Great Depression" shattered hopes of a regional economic revival based on renewed industrial development or new resource processing. The total value of exports dropped by 27%, as the regional economy suffered from a series of world-wide price drops. Newsprint prices dropped by 35% between 1928 and 1934; and fish prices were halved. Timber output dropped by a quarter; and fish, farm and coal output fell by nearly half, as resource sectors were "rationalized" and forced to adjust to lessening demand. At the same time, manufacturing output shrank more than 60%. One of the few sectors that expanded capacity during the twenties and thirties was the pulp and paper industry. A number of new communities sprang up in Nova Scotia, New Brunswick and Newfoundland to serve its demands.[17]

By 1933, debt servicing consumed between one-third and one-half of Nova Scotia's and New Brunswick's revenues. With little local capital or profits available to invest in renewing the region's hard-pressed urban infrastructure, there was little hope for a revival of hard-pressed towns and cities. Retailing, increasingly controlled from central Canada, was one of the few urban-based growth sectors. Moncton, one of the few towns that experienced much growth during this period, expanded its tertiary sectors, a result of the expansion of branch-business retail outlets, and retained some of its manufacturing core because of its Canadian National Railway shops. Pictou and Amherst never recovered from the post-war recession that saw their manufacturing sectors cut by half. Sydney's massive steel plant was cut back drastically but continued in operation for the period (see Fig. II.2).[18]

Relations," M.A. Thesis, University of New Brunswick, 1980; and Forbes, *Maritime Rights…*

17. S.A. Saunders, *The Economic History of the Maritime Provinces since Confederation* (Fredericton, 1984) [1939]; Alexander, "Economic Growth in the Atlantic Region…"; Peter Neary, *Newfoundland in the North Atlantic World, 1929–1949* (Montreal/Kingston, 1988); L.Anders Sandberg, "Introduction: Dependent Development and Client States: Forest Policy and Social Conflict in Nova Scotia and New Brunswick," in *Trouble in the Woods: Forest Policy and Social Conflict in Nova Scotia and New Brunswick,* L. Anders Sandberg (ed.) (Fredericton, 1992); Bill Parenteau, "The Woods Transformed: The Emergence of the Pulp and Paper Industry in New Brunswick, 1918–1931," in *Acadiensis* XXII, 1 (Autumn, 1992); on Newfoundland see James Hiller, "The Origins of the Pulp and Paper Industry in Newfoundland," in *Acadiensis* XI, 2 (Spring, 1982); and "The Politics of Newsprint: The Newfoundland Pulp and Paper Industry, 1915–1939," in *Acadiensis* XIX, 2 (Spring, 1990).

18. L.D. McCann, "Metropolitanism and Branch Businesses in the Maritimes, 1881–1931," in *Acadiensis* XIII, 1 (Autumn, 1983); and L.D. McCann, "Industrialization in the Maritimes [Plate 25], *Historical Atlas of Canada, Vol. III, Addressing the 20th Century,* Donald Kerr and Deryck W. Holdsworth (eds.) (Toronto, 1990); see also David Frank, "The 1920s: Class, Region, Resistance and Accommodation"; and E.R. Forbes, "The 1930s: Depression and Retrenchment," both in *The Atlantic Provinces in Confederation,* E.R. Forbes and D.A. Muise (eds.) (Toronto, 1993).

Figure II.2   Loss of manufacturing jobs in selected towns, 1912–31

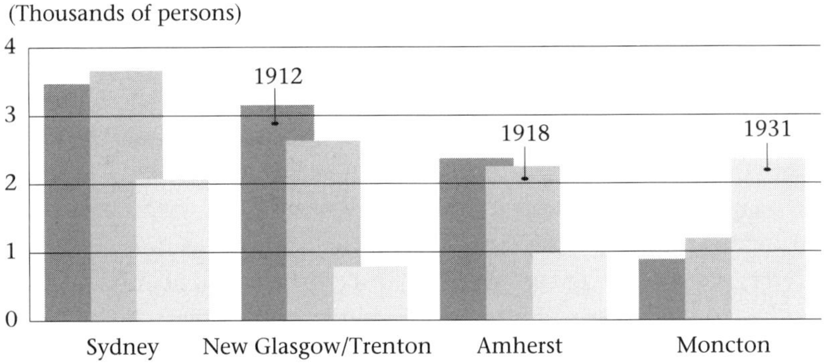

(Thousands of persons)

Total number of workers: 1912=10,092; 1918=9,748; 1931=5,640.

In the vortex of the depression, local governments could do little to remedy the social and economic implications of urban decline for their unemployed workers. Those few factories and coal mines that continued to operate, mostly on some sort of a part time basis, demanded further austerity from their workers to compensate for declining profit margins. They fell behind with their tax bills, as did unemployed workers faced with declining incomes. Municipalities accumulated huge debts to maintain infrastructures and services in the face of dwindling tax bases. Responsibility for relief increased the already immense debt loads of towns during the Depression. Many municipalities were unable to supply adequate relief to the unemployed, as taxes became harder to collect and loans more difficult to obtain. Provincial governments, struggling with their own fiscal problems, found it difficult to assist their municipalities, some of which even gave up their corporate status during the hungry thirties.[19]

Newfoundland's situation was especially desperate, since municipal government was virtually absent there and much of its existing debt was to outside creditors. The Dominion government in St. John's bore full responsibility for relief payments to the most destitute. Concern on the part of Canada's and Britain's governments, both with considerable financial and constitutional stakes in Newfoundland's fiscal health, led to replacement of responsible government by an appointed commission of government in 1934. For Newfoundlanders, the loss of democratic institutions was accompanied by poverty, unemployment, and the humiliation of dependence on government relief administered by agencies that were not even a part of their own constitutional establishment.[20]

19. Ernest R. Forbes, "Cutting the Pie into Smaller Pieces: Matching Grants and Relief in the Maritime Provinces During the 1930s," in *Acadiensis* XVII, 1 (Autumn 1987).

World War II pushed economic considerations to a secondary position as both the Canadian and Newfoundland governments assumed sweeping powers to direct a "win-the-war" strategy. Strategically important to the "Battle of the Atlantic", Newfoundland now experienced the greatest prosperity in its history. Military personnel from Canada and the United States built bases and local community structures across the Island. The United States government acquired military bases at St. John's, Argentia, and Stephenville; Canada set up air bases at Gander, in central Newfoundland, and at Goose Bay, in Labrador. By 1941, Newfoundland had achieved near full employment, where a few years earlier there had been widespread social dislocation. 20,000

Fort Needam Park temporary wartime housing, Halifax, 1943 The pressures brought on by the arrival of so many young people forced authorities to provide housing, an intervention by the federal government that would have important echoes in the post-war era. So-called temporary buildings overlooking Halifax harbour were commonplace across the country at the time; many would continue to in use long after the war was over. *Source: Public Archives of Nova Scotia.*

Newfoundlanders, approximately 20% of the entire adult male workforce, were employed in construction jobs associated with the boom. Fifteen thousand Canadian and American military personnel were stationed in the St. John's area alone. Halifax was even more dramatically transformed, as tens of thousands of soldiers, sailors and airmen, along with their families in some instances, flooded through the port. Smaller military bases were scattered throughout the Maritimes and they affected their immediate areas in a similar manner.[21]

---

20. Alexander, "Economic Growth in the Atlantic Region…"; Neary, *Newfoundland in the North Atlantic World*…; and James Overton, "Economic Crisis and the End of Democracy: Politics in Newfoundland During the Great Depression," *Labour/Le Travail* 26 (Fall, 1990).

21. Neary, *Newfoundland in the North Atlantic World*…; Malcolm MacLeod, *Peace of the Continent: The Impact of Second World War Canadian and American Bases in Newfoundland* (St. John's, 1986); Carman Miller, "The 1940s: War and Rehabilitation," in *The Atlantic Provinces in Confederation*…, Forbes and Muise (eds.); J. White, "The Home Front: The Accommodation Crisis in Halifax, 1941–1951," in *Urban History Review/Revue d'histoire urbaine* 20, 3 (February, 1992).

Across the Maritimes, wartime stresses were substantial, especially for towns and cities, whose basic infrastructures of streets, sewers and water systems were in desperate condition following two decades of recession. Halifax, full of sailors and soldiers awaiting embarkation for Europe or the North Atlantic, became a tense, overcrowded community. But industrial centres had work again, and vessels filled ports across the region. Munition manufacture and ship-repair brought renewed activity to Pictou's steel towns, as well as to Saint John and Halifax. Cotton mills at Marysville, Milltown, Yarmouth, Windsor and Truro all produced at capacity again and munitions factories were operating in several communities.

The basis of the new economic structure was to be state intervention. Yet, federally designed wartime production policies deliberately bypassed the region's heavier industries in favour of fostering industrial growth elsewhere in Canada. Some factories in the region were brought back into production as part of the war effort. But C.D. Howe's vision of a developed post-war Canada failed to include an industrialized Maritimes. In the long term, failure to plant more of the war industries there weakened Maritime manufacturing and reinforced central Canada's economic dominance. Federal policies favoured shipbuilding at St. Lawrence and Great Lakes yards using steel plate from Hamilton, rather than at Saint John and Halifax shipyards which might have used Sydney or Trenton produced steel.[22]

When war ended in 1945 the Department of National Defence would be pressured to maintain a military presence throughout the region for economic purposes rather for the defense against immediate threat. Air bases, which had so transformed Summerside and Greenwood during the war, would continue to have an impact after the war ended. The consequences of continuing to have a major naval headquarters in Halifax was pervasive, as the city took on the attributes of a military centre of great significance. Expansion of Camp Gagetown in New Brunswick in the 1950s created the nearby town of Oromocto to house the families of servicemen, a carefully planned community that stood in contrast to older towns in the region (see Fig. II.3).

As military expenditure and war-related activity declined, numerous studies were commissioned at both provincial and federal levels to recommend a direction for post-war development. Implicit in these so called *"Reconstruction"* studies was a concern that the wartime boom

22. Ernest R. Forbes, "Consolidating Disparity: The Maritimes and the Industrialization of Canada during the Second World War," in *Acadiensis* XV, 2 (Spring, 1986): 3-27; R.A. Young, "'And the People will sink into despair': Reconstruction in New Brunswick, 1942–52," in *Canadian Historical Review* LXIX (June, 1988); and Christopher A. Sharpe and Lynne Marks, "The Home Front in the Second World War" [Plate 48], in *Historical Atlas of Canada*…

might dissipate as quickly as it had formed, leaving behind economic distress that had brought so much grief to the regional economy following World War I, two decades earlier. Everywhere, the conclusion was that a much more active set of state policies would be necessary to ensure a prosperous future. While central Canada's economy leapt forward in the immediate post-war years based on the initiatives that had

Figure II.3   Urban population rate in Canada and the Atlantic provinces, 1921–91

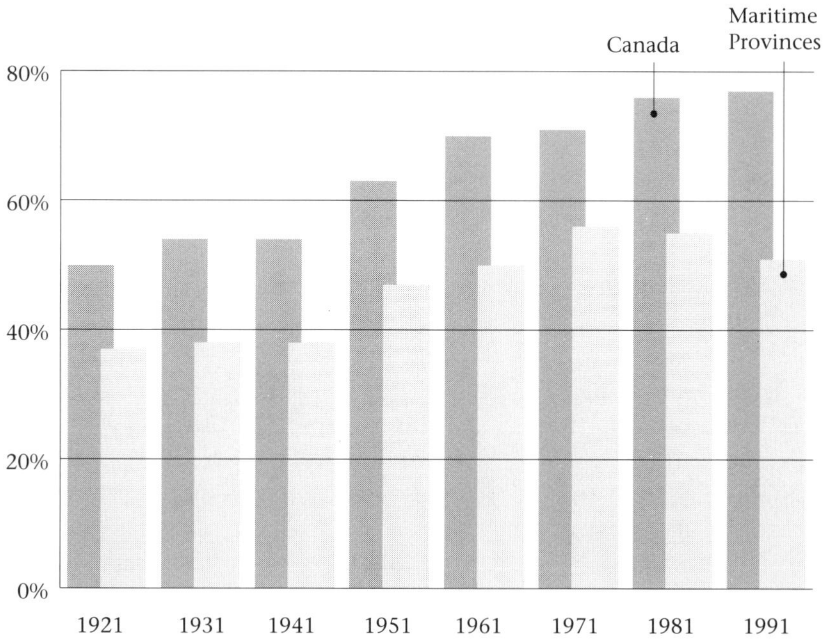

Source: Census Canada (Newfoundland included only after 1949).

been taken during the war, Maritimers found only limited options. In the expectation of federal assistance, long-needed public works, such as roads, sewers, and other infrastructure improvements, were planned. Planners also envisaged an expansion of health and education, and services such as rural electrification.[23]

Newfoundlanders emerged from war facing a difficult decision regarding their political future. Full employment and the virtual elimination of the public debt had forced a reconsideration of the commission of government. Britain's new Labour government was

23. Young, "And the People will sink into Despair..."; Robert Bothwell, Ian Drummond and John English, *Canada Since 1945: Power, Politics and Provincialism* (Toronto, 1981).

determined to divest itself of direct responsibility for governing far away colonies. The decision to join Canada in 1949, following a long and acrimonious debate, was made with the expectation that the Canadian government would use its financial strength to promote development and provide social services to cushion Newfoundlanders from the vagaries of their dependence on a single staple. The main lines of the debate focused on appeals to modernity and the ability to influence the affairs of the Dominion. Opposition to union by St. John's merchants signaled their unwillingness to see outside interests interfere with their traditional position of power. The 1949 decision set off profound social and economic transformations change across all aspects of Newfoundland society, a process that would challenge the foundations of communities so long dependent on the fishery.

The 1950s to the Present

Recommendations for increased financial support for fiscally-strapped provinces were implemented only piece-meal during the decade following the war. The government of Louis St Laurent provided assistance for national construction projects such as the Trans-Canada Highway, and developed new policies for airport construction all across the Dominion. A National Housing Act created the Central Mortgage and Housing Corporation to assist construction of thousands of new urban and suburban homes. All these initiatives would have important implications for urban renewal projects across the region, eventually even prompting development of a more systematic approach to urban planning.

This preoccupation with delivery of services as a precondition for economic expansion was extended in the 1950s to the task of economic development as both the federal and provincial levels of government sought to combat the economic decay of the region. The result marked a decisive change in the political economy of the region. As governments addressed deteriorating economic conditions across the region, they experimented with a "political-economy of management" which replaced laissez-faire with direct state intervention.[24]

Continued stagnation of the region's manufacturing sector during the 1950s rankled all the more, given the economic advances of central and western Canada. In time, a complex system of transfer payments from federal to provincial governments was developed to assist with the delivery of essential services. The Royal Commission on Canada's Economic Prospects (1957), presided over by Toronto-based economist Walter Gordon, acknowledged the federal government's

---

24. Margaret Conrad, "The Atlantic Revolution of the 1950s," in *Beyond Anger and Longing: Community Development in Atlantic Canada,* Berkeley Fleming (ed.) (Fredericton, 1988); T.J. O'Neill, *Educator, Advocate and Critic, APEC's First 25 Year* (Halifax, 1979).

responsibility, within certain limits, to assist in regional economic development. Since it was deemed unacceptable to manipulate tariff levels that might result in discrimination against specific regions, the main thrust of the federal government was directed to transportation and compensatory benefits. One consequence of this was that towns and cities deemed to have suffered from relative underdevelopment during preceding decades, became eligible for grants to encourage the infrastructure development necessary to attract new industries to the region's towns.[25]

The Conservative government of John G. Diefenbaker,

Gulf Oil refinery, Port Hawkesbury, ca 1975
Transformation of previously under-industrialized areas characterized the period of "Political Economy of Management." Massive and expensive industries featured transfer of readily available technologies, encouraged by governments determined to force development. Sometimes results were not altogether satisfactory for the communities affected. The physical changes were enormous, but environmental implications have yet to be adequately measured and the tendency to alienate large blocks of prime resources or well placed land was common-place. *Source: Nova Scotia Information Services.*

which came into office in 1956, supported regional development, though it stopped short of direct aid for the creation of industries in Atlantic Canada. Provincial governments also took an active role in attracting industry by such means as highway construction and land

25. F. Homer Zwicker, *Royal Commission Reports and Related Action* (Halifax, 1960); James Bickerton, *Nova Scotia, Ottawa and the Politics of Regional Development* (Toronto, 1990).

assembly, as well as through bonuses and tax incentives of one sort or another. Nova Scotia's Industrial Estates Corporation was typical of provincial agencies created to assist development by creating equity funds for luring capitalists to come to the region. All four Atlantic provinces attempted similar initiatives, which had an impact on those towns that were designated as most likely to host new industries.[26]

Both the federal and provincial governments initiated a number of mega-projects designed to build and strengthen infrastructures within the region. In 1955, the Canso Causeway, funded jointly by the federal and provincial governments, replaced the outmoded car and railway ferry system operated by Canadian National Railways, finally joining the rest of Nova Scotia to Cape Breton Island. An immediate result was the emergence of a new urban growth centre at Port Hawkesbury. The new harbour created by the causeway provided a site for a pulp mill, a heavy water plant, and an oil refinery. The Beechwood Power development in Northern New Brunswick was designed to prompt the same sort of development there, though it was specifically designed to initiate the base metals industry in the process of evolving.[27]

A new highway around Bedford Basin and the Angus L. MacDonald Bridge across the harbour narrows opened the near hinterland of both Halifax with Dartmouth and led to direct incorporation of a number of outlying areas into metropolitan functions. This process would be extended by relocation and expansion of Halifax's international airport and completion of a circumferential highway linking the city to surrounding communities over the ensuing decades. The significance of transportation improvements such as these, which were replicated to varying degrees in Saint John and St. John's, was that they permitted people to live farther than ever before from their workplaces. This was typical of the second phase of suburbanization then occurring across North America.[28]

The Atlantic Provinces Economic Council (APEC), an independent body created by the provincial governments in 1954, criticized the uncoordinated and ad-hoc nature of federal government

26. James Bickerton, *Nova Scotia, Ottawa and the Politics of Regional Development* …; Gerhard P. Bassler, "'Develop or Perish': Joseph R. Smallwood and Newfoundland's Quest for German Industry, 1949–1953," in *Acadiensis* XV, 2 (Spring, 1986); Roy E. George, *A Leader and a Laggard: Manufacturing industry in Nova Scotia, Quebec and Ontario* (Toronto, 1970).

27. R.L. Foote, *The Case of Port Hawkesbury: Rapid Industrialization and Social Unrest in a Nova Scotia Community* (Toronto, 1979); James Kenny, "Politics and Persistence: New Brunswick's Hugh John Flemming and the 'Atlantic Revolution' 1952–1960," unpublished M.A. Thesis, University of New Brunswick, 1988.

28. David Boucher, "Metropolitan Growth in Atlantic Canada: The Saint John Throughwa," unpublished M.A. Thesis (Canadian Studies), Carleton University, 1993.

expenditures. APEC, acting basically as spokesperson for the business classes of the region, favoured development of regional infrastructures as the most promising type of involvement by the federal government.[29] In 1962, the Atlantic Development Board (ADB) was established by the federal government to coordinate industrial development. Its purpose was to avoid duplication of effort in programs designed to address problems of chronic underemployment. The Fund for Rural Economic Development (FRED) was also created in the early 1960s.

In 1969, Prince Edward Island's government negotiated the region's largest administrative experiment – the Provincial Development Plan. The Plan created a permanent federal/provincial bureaucracy to oversee development and monitor expenditures of the federal and provincial governments on the Island. Within a decade, two-thirds of all economic activity on the Island was generated from these joint expenditures. It reflected an enormous commitment on the part of both levels of government to effectively manage Island resources. While the basic thrust of the Plan was to be better management of the farming/fishing and tourism industries, it had profound implications for Charlottetown, which attracted more and more Islanders to its outskirts in search of the many new jobs in the burgeoning bureaucracy.[30]

Arrival of the Trudeau government, in 1968, marked a changed approach towards regional development. With the realization that an agency was needed to coordinate government programs already in place, the Department of Regional Economic Expansion (DREE) was created. Though not exclusively focused on Atlantic Canada, DREE had much involvement there, concentrating its expenditures on industrial growth poles, often in existing urban centres. The hope was that the effects of development there would trickle down to outlying areas. In turn, outlying areas would assist towns and cities by supplying resources and a mobile and flexible labour force.[31] DREE's concentration on growth poles was designed to halt urban population decline and bolster economic development. Between 1974 and 1981, major

29. The Atlantic Provinces Economic Council is a free-standing advisory group – supported by the federal and all four provincial governments – to provide an independent viewpoint on development decisions. See T.J. O'Neill, *Educator, Advocate and Critics…*; R.L. McAllister, "Canadian Program Experiences," in *Regional Economic Policy*, N.H. Lithwick (ed.) (Toronto, 1978); and James Bickerton, "Regional Policy in Historical Perspective," in *An Analysis of the Reorganization for Economic Development* (Halifax, 1982).
30. Donald Nemetz, "Managing Development," in *The Garden Transformed: Prince Edward Island, 1945–1980*, Verner Smitheram, David Milne and Satadal Dasgupta (eds.) (Charlottetown, 1982).
31. Bickerton, "Regional Policy in Historical Perspective…" For a more personal perspective see Tom Kent, "The Brief Rise and Early Decline of Regional Development," in *Acadiensis* IX, 1 (Autumn, 1979).

urban renewal projects included the Historic Properties and waterfront development in Halifax, Confederation Centre in Charlottetown, and Market Square in Saint John. In St. John's, a major harbour redevelopment project that had started modestly in 1956 was completed in 1965, when port facilities were modernized under a federal nationalization scheme. In addition a number of industrial parks with serviced land and favourable terms for development were created across the entire region with funds made available by both federal and provincial governments.

Canada's centennial celebrations in 1967 included a number of major initiatives in heritage related developments, which coincided with restoration of Fortress Louisbourg, one of the sops offered by the federal government to the declining coal mining communities of industrial Cape Breton. Over the ensuing years the federal and provincial governments would collaborate in developing a number of other large historic sites and parks, all of which were designed to attract tourists to the region. Hand-in-hand with these major redevelopment schemes was renewed interest in the preservation of regional heritage architecture as a means of tourist development. In the 1970s and 1980s, tourism would become the most important single industry in the region. While the natural environment was always the region's greatest attraction, culture has been prominently featured in strategies to attract tourist dollars to urban areas.[32]

Provincial and municipal government reform also had an impact on urban development during this era. New Brunswick's new Equal Opportunity Program, designed to reduce inequality between regions of the province and standardize the educational, social and welfare services offered by municipalities, emerged from the 1963 Royal Commission on Finance and Municipal Taxation (Byrne Commission). In Nova Scotia, a complete over-haul of the municipal legislation, a course recommended by yet another provincial commission on the reform of municipal government (The Graham Commission), was motivated by the same perceived inequalities. A by-product of both initiatives was the reorganization of various municipalities into regional authorities, with funding and control of such basic services as health and education centralized under the influence or control of provincial governments. Another effect was extensive re-drawing of municipal boundaries that has important bearings on classification of urban/ rural qualities in the post-1960 censuses.[33]

32. Ian McKay, "Tartanism Triumphant: The Construction of Scottishness in Nova Scotia, 1933–1954," in *Acadiensis* XXI, 2 (Spring, 1992)

33. Della M. M. Stanley, *Louis Robichaud: A Decade of Power* (Halifax, 1984); John F. Grahame, *Provincial-municipal Relations in the Maritime Provinces* (Fredericton, 1970);

These programs clearly reflected the growing commitment of the state to developing strategies for economic recovery. The role of governments continued to grow when a new Department of Regional Industrial Expansion (DRIE), reporting directly to cabinet, was created after the dismantling of DREE in 1981.[34] DRIE operated for five years until it was replaced in 1987 by the Atlantic Canada Opportunities Agency (ACOA), with a mission to "rekindle" the entrepreneurial spirit of the region. A consequence of these various government programs, all aimed at equalizing regional disparities across the country, has been to consolidate power and authority in the region's metropolitan centres. Halifax and St. John's, for instance, by the continued buoyancy of their economies, relative to the rest of the region, have been provided with the retail hinterlands they lacked earlier in the century.

Moncton and Halifax have been the fastest growing cities in the region over the past two decades, largely because of their administrative and commercial functions within the broad strategy of regional renewal. Moncton serves as the commercial and public service hub for southeastern New Brunswick and northern Nova Scotia, as well as for Prince Edward Islanders, who take advantage of improved ferry connections between Borden and nearby Cape Tormentine. A major factor in this urban revival is the location in the community of a number of federal government offices, including ACOA, that take advantage of the city's central location and bilingual population.

This process of consolidating the dominance of a few cities has been assisted by expenditures on various road construction projects and by various federal/provincial urban renewal schemes aimed at reinforcing core areas in designated centres of growth. The danger of dependence on combinations of external politicians and capitalists is that industries and agencies attracted to communities by special concessions are in a position to dictate their terms for continuing to operate. The possibility of governments withdrawing offices or programs from the region during times of fiscal restraint has proved as worrisome a threat as the tendency of capitalists to "rationalize" their operations by withdrawing from the region.[35]

---

and John F. Graham, *Report of the Royal Commission in Education, Public Services and Provincial Municipal Relations* (Halifax, 1974).

34. Donald J. Savoie, *Federal-provincial collaboration: The Canada-New Brunswick General Development Agreement* (Ottawa, 1981); and *Regional Economic Development: Canada's Search for Solutions* (second edition) (Toronto, 1992).

35. E.R. Forbes, "The Atlantic Provinces, Free Trade and the Canadian Constitution," in *Challenging the Regional Stereotype* (Fredericton, 1990); and David Alexander, "New Notions of Happiness: Nationalism, Regionalism and Atlantic Canada," in *Atlantic Canada and Confederation: Essays in Canadian Political Economy,* Eric W. Sager, Lewis R. Fisher and Stuart O. Pierson (eds.) (Toronto, 1983).

Federal and provincial government takeovers of Cape Breton's coal mines and steel mill following the withdrawal of capitalists in the mid-1960s are extreme examples of this sort of intervention. Insufficient profits had been cited as the reason for withdrawal from declining communities surrounding Sydney harbour by these outside-based capitalists. The federal and provincial governments reluctantly stepped in, ostensibly to regulate social implications of the massive dislocations that would be a consequence of closures. The result has been a major experimentation in public ownership of the largest industrial establishment in the region. While the take-over was predicated on reducing the size and scope of the work-force in a systematic and socially responsible fashion, the effect has been a

Heavy water plant at Glace Bay, 1971
Still under construction in this photo, the Deuterium Heavy Water Plant was an example of state planning without much consideration for local impact. The plant, like so many modern installations, was located far from the core of the community and featured a huge parking lot as one of its central aspects. As well, like so many of the mega-projects initiated in the region, it was an abject failure. *Source: Public Archives of Nova Scotia*

disaster for the communities involved and all attempts at replacement have fallen on hard times. In this case, government intervention was seen as a last resort, but all manner of intermediate levels of control over economic development or over resource management have continued to have a decisive impact on regional communities.[36]

Smaller yet equally critical consolidations have relied on federal and provincial programs to launch capital development or to restructure the region's staple industries of the region, many characterized by political rather than economic considerations in critical decision-making. The fish processing industry in all four provinces had functioned for centuries without much new investment or direct involvement by government, but required centralized processing facilities to compete

36. Joan Bishop, "Sydney Steel: Public Ownership and the Welfare State, 1967–1975," in *The Island: New Perspectives on Cape Breton's History, 1713–1990,* Kenneth Donovan (ed.) (Fredericton, 1990);

in international markets. New plants and equipment were installed across the region, with massive assistance from federal and provincial governments. As a spin-off, a number of programs for redeveloping the fishery itself have been undertaken, with what appear to be disastrous results for communities directly dependent on that industry. The result has been concentration of control into fewer and fewer corporations, whose domination extends not only processing the fish, but to gathering it as well.

Mammoth new potato processing facilities in Prince Edward Island and New Brunswick have produced similar restructuring of these industries. Cavendish Farms, controlled by the Irving family, and the McCain's interests, now manage vast areas of the region's agricultural economy, and have forced a restructuring of the provision of services in smaller communities.[37] This new "Political Economy of Management" has had a dramatic impact on people's everyday lives, as well as on the economic activity within communities.

Periods of political and economic change have featured various levels of state intervention in the formation of urban systems. In the process, towns and cities in Atlantic Canada have emerged from their more limited status in the mercantile system. Their passage through the somewhat tumultuous industrial era had been brief and the implications of the modern service-oriented economy of the current era are still to be felt.

37. Richard Apostle and Gene Barratt, *Emptying Their Nets: Small Capital and Rural Industrialization in the Nova Scotia Fishing Industry* (Toronto, 1992); "The Fisheries," a special issue of the *Journal of Canadian Studies* 19, 1 (Spring, 1984); see as well Martha MacDonald and Patricia Connelly, "A Leaner, Meaner Industry: A Case Study of 'Restructuring,' in the Nova Scotia Fishery"; and Thomas R. Murphy, "From Family Farming to Capitalist Agriculture: Food Production, Agribusiness and the State," both in Fairly et. al. (eds.), *Restructuring and Resistance*....

Chapter III

Farm and Fishing Villages: Zones of Persistent Rurality

Less than one third of populations in rural districts live in towns or cities. Usually, such districts achieve lower population gains than those where towns play a more decisive role in community development. As rural areas reached demographic crisis in the mid-nineteenth century, their subsistence farming was incapable of providing the sort of economic opportunities needed to stem the tide of out-migration, so that, in some instances, rates of depopulation have been high. Such areas appear structurally incapable of generating sufficient surpluses to attract the sort of inter-generational economic growth needed to sustain the development of modern social institutions in their communities.[1]

Rural regions may differ widely in economic orientation and social background, but their urban/rural profiles seldom vary much over time. For the purposes of our analysis, these less urbanized zones have been divided into *coastal littorals* and *farming areas*.[2] The latter tend to be more densely populated than the former. The original staple of most littoral areas was fish, with farming and/or forestry pursued on a subsistence or seasonal basis by their inhabitants. Farming areas often had some seasonal dependence on forestry or fishing as well. For areas where outputs in all sectors of the economy remained at subsistence levels, it is difficult to determine if it was more directed towards one

1. Marvin McInnis, "Migration"; "Elements of Population Change"; and "The Demographic Transition" [Plates 27, 28, 29], in *Historical Atlas of Canada, Volume III: Addressing the Twentieth Century, 1891–1961,* Donald Kerr and Deryck W. Holdsworth (eds.) (Toronto, 1990).
2. *Coastal littorals* are thinly populated areas whose towns serve as gathering and distribution points for fish and timber. Populations in *Agricultural Districts* produce surpluses for sale. Frequently residents in either zone pursue other occupations might on a seasonal basis to supplement farm or fishing income.

activity or the another, so geography became a more important consideration in our decisions about where to situate a particular census district. In some cases their experience has varied across time, responding to changing economic circumstances.

In spite of some changes in their populations, with a few exceptions even the largest towns in these districts seldom exceed 5,000 people; the majority have between 1,000 and 2,000. But even where new industries have produced economic booms of a sort in recent years, workers often adjust to new labour demands without major population redistribution. Indeed, since 1950, investment in newer resource processing facilities within these zones has not resulted in as much restructuring of the population as one might imagine.

The central political objective of most such economic initiatives appears to have been maintenance of communities facing underemployment and out-migration. Often the solutions exploit the economic weakness of rural areas, attempting to halt the exodus of surplus labour to more expansive sectors of the Canadian economy by various forms of incentives to encourage the location of jobs within existing communities. Other interventions in the form of improved infrastructures help older communities to survive, sometimes contributing to persistence of rural norms within the region. This seeming contradiction reflects adaptive strategies by rural-based residents as they search for employment and services.

The most prevalent characteristic of these rural areas is the service and distribution nature of local town economies. Towns which previously served as centres for gathering produce and distributing consumer goods, now serve as postal, medical, educational and retail centres for a widening arch of surrounding rural communities. These functions seldom require large numbers of urban workers. Their working populations tend as often as not to live in surrounding rural areas, rather than in the shadow of the new factories, as was the case during the industrial boom that impacted on the region during the earlier part of the century. In fact, the newer factories are often located on the outskirts of towns, where land and services can be assembled and where the "Political Economy of Management" can have free reign from the political interference of local businessmen and tax structures.

Agricultural Districts

Prince Edward Island, the Annapolis-Kings-Hants-Colchester region of central Nova Scotia, and New Brunswick's Saint John Valley all experienced parallel settlement patterns. All three areas are made up predominantly of people of British/American stock whose ancestors came to the region in the late eighteenth century, when they took over lands previously improved by the Acadians, who had been expelled during the conflict between the British and French. An anomaly to this trend is Madawaska County, at the headwaters of the Saint John River, where Acadians make up a majority, and where farming is less well established as a primary industry than elsewhere.

Even though geographical settings and to some extent their products can vary considerably all three districts has a similar economic base. While much of Prince Edward Island's land is devoted to farming, smaller urban centres along its coasts functioned as shipbuilding centres at various times. In addition they provided farmers with a wide range of services and acted as focal points for an evolving inshore fishery that on the Island has specifically local and seasonal dimensions.

The coastal communities of Charlotte County in New Brunswick and parts of Kings and Hants counties in Nova Scotia served similar economic functions, building ships and exporting timber during the lumber's hey-day, even though most residents there continued to call themselves farmers. While agricultural production and related food processing have been central throughout all three regions, residents also occasionally supplement farming with migrations to nearby or distant urban areas for waged employment. But since completion of the settlement process, about the middle of the nineteenth century, these mature areas of the region have experienced successive demographic crises.

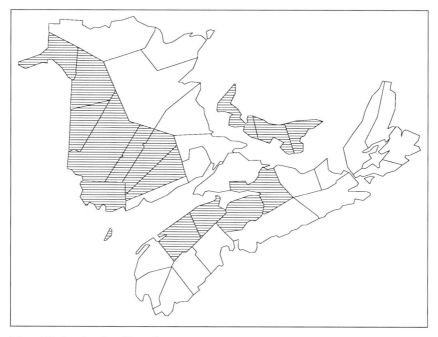

Map III.1   Agricultural zones

New Brunswick

The Saint John River has always dominated New Brunswick's agricultural heartland.[3] Not only was it a vital means of transport, but its wide intervale and upland areas include much of the province's choicest farm lands. Communities located there depended on the city of Saint John, which is contained within a narrow census district of its own stretching along the Bay of Fundy at the mouth of the river and outside the bounds of the agricultural area described here. The river valley contains a number of important towns and cities, which grew very little prior to World War II, a period when urban/rural ratios remained by and large constant. The major development prior to 1900 was the establishment of Marysville – on the Nashwaak River near Fredericton – and the development of Milltown, on the outskirts of Saint Stephen, in Charlotte County. Both experienced similar bursts of growth during the *National Policy* era as lumbering and cotton milling towns.

Most post-1951 urban growth in the Saint John Valley has centred on Fredericton, where the population increased threefold

Saint Stephen/Milltown, ca 1910
The fully equipped industrial town featured a number of new technologies. Saint Stephen, much like others across the region, installed these systems as quickly as they became available. Electric streetcars and paved streets, along with telephones, water and sewer services, were all expensive for the new municipal governments anxious to appear as up-to-date as possible in the competition for new capital investments. The second photo shows the huge cotton mill located just up-river from Saint Stephen at Milltown, a development characteristic of the region's fragmented industrial development. *Source: Provincial Archives of New Brunswick*

3.   Included in New Brunswick's agricultural area are the counties of Carleton, Charlotte, Kings, Madawaska, Queens, Sunbury, Victoria and York. Recent expansion in Kings County's population, largely a consequence of the spread of Saint John's suburbs northward, distorts the urban/rural ratios slightly.

from about 16,000 to 46,000. While Fredericton's economic role in the valley was always auxiliary to that of Saint John, it remained important as a distributing centre as well as for its governmental functions. Early in the nineteenth century, numerous water and steam-powered sawmills were located within the city, which also served as a service and distribution centre for the upper river valley.[4] Prominence as an administrative and educational centre has increased with the growth of the provincial government and expansion of the University of New Brunswick. The town of Oromocto, established when Gagetown became a military base, is an integral part of Fredericton's urban network; as is Marysville, whose huge nineteenth century cotton mill, abandoned for much of this century, has been retro-fitted for government offices.

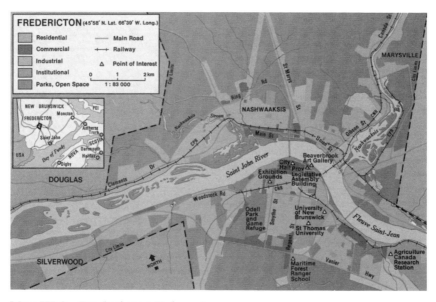

Map III.2   Fredericton Urban Area

Overall, the Saint John Valley's rural population has remained relatively stable since 1871, about 120,000. Though productivity of farms has increased dramatically in recent years, a decrease in the number of family farms has occurred, particularly in the potato growing areas up river from Fredericton and in the dairy areas of the Sussex region. This process, part of a consolidation of the agricultural sector into the hands of a few of larger processors, is also a consequence of improvements to transportation that permit faster and more efficient

4.   W. Austin Squires, *History of Fredericton: The Last 200 Years* (Fredericton, 1980).

delivery of produce for processing. The emergence of a number of inter-dependent processing towns such as Florenceville and Hartland, part of the McCain empire of the Upper Saint John Valley, make processing agricultural produce a more centralized industry than ever before.[5]

Figure III.1   Urban/rural population change in New Brunswick farming areas, 1871–1991

(Thousands of persons)

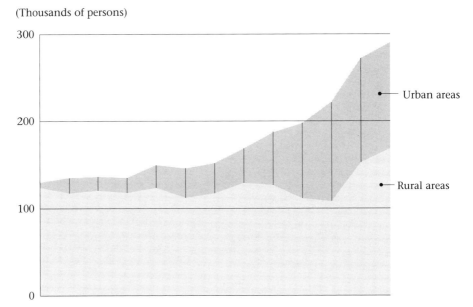

Of the primary industries besides farming, forestry has experienced the most dramatic development since 1920, though lumber exports have declined steadily as a proportion of the forest-based industries since 1900. From that time onward the growth sector has been pulp and paper making rather than lumber. New and expanded towns developed wherever large mills were established. Construction of the Fraser Company's huge pulp mill there prompted Edmundston's emergence as a sub-regional metropolitan centre. Between 1911 and 1931, its population almost quadrupled, from 1,821 to 6,430. And since then, it has grown to more than 12,000.[6]

5.   Murphy, "From Family Farming to Capitalist Agriculture…"
6.   Nicole Lang, "L'impact d'une industrie: Les effets sociaux de l'arrivée de la compagnie Fraser Limited à Edmundston, N.-B., 1900–1950," in *Revue de la Société historique de Madawaska* XV, 1-2 (Jan–Juin, 1987).

While Edmundston acts as a service centre for the surrounding farming communities, it remains a city built around its pulp and paper mill, whose presence contributes to the stability of the rural population as well. The seasonal nature of the labour force needed to harvest and move timber, permits many farmers to remain on marginal land. Pulp mills are also located in Saint John, and at St. George's in Charlotte County.

Nova Scotia And Prince Edward Island

Demographic patterns of farm districts in Nova Scotia and Prince Edward Island parallel New Brunswick's.[7] Charlottetown, situated on an excellent harbour at the mouth of the Hillsborough River near the centre of Prince Edward Island functions as a commercial entrepot as well as a political capital. While it grew by 30% between 1871 and 1881, a decade when provincial totals increased at only half that rate.

Figure III.2   Urban/rural population change in Nova Scotia and Prince Edward Island farming areas, 1871–1991

(Thousands of persons)

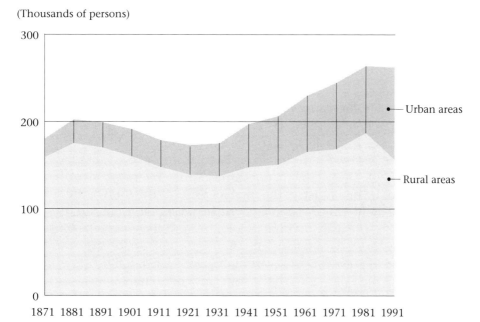

Towns: Bridgetown, Wolfville, Kentville, Windsor, Hantsport, Truro, Charlottetown, Summerside.

7.   Included in the Nova Scotia-Prince Edward Island farming districts are: Prince, Kings and Queens counties in Prince Edward Island, and Annapolis, Kings, Hants and Colchester in Nova Scotia. The urban/rural profile of the two is quite similar. Combining the two areas produces a population approximating New Brunswick's agricultural areas.

Neither Charlottetown's nor the province's population would grow appreciably during the next hundred years. Recently, though the city proper has decreased in population, its suburbs are growing rapidly. Now upwards of half of all Islanders live within a short commuting distance of the capital.

The four counties of the Annapolis Valley/Colchester section of Nova Scotia, referred to in part at least as the Western counties, lack the major political nucleus provided by cities such as Charlottetown or Fredericton. But the area has been served by railways since the mid-nineteenth century, when it was swept into the commercial orbit of Halifax. Truro emerged as its largest town, with a manufacturing base in textiles and furniture, a significant educational establishment with the provincial teachers college and an agricultural college. It also serves as a service centre for the rich farming communities of the area and as a railway hub for west-bound trains from Cape Breton, Halifax and the western counties.

Through the Annapolis Valley, towns are spaced out to provide services to farmers. Windsor and Kentville specialize in marketing and processing the output of the rich apple farms, which enjoyed a large export market from time to time, though a large market gardening sector is linked into major Halifax markets.[8] The air base at Greenwood and the naval training station at Cornwallis anchor the southern end of the valley, which is also its most rural area. These military bases contribute to the survival of these communities by providing secure employment for many workers from the surrounding country-side. At the other end of the valley Acadia University, located at Wolfville has expanded to make it one of the largest employers in the area.

Since 1941, both the urban and rural sectors of the valley have experienced steady growth, reflecting a strong interdependence between the two. Some of the rural increase is a function of the emergence of more densely populated fringes areas on the outskirts of established towns. Most rural residents were fully or partially integrated within adjacent towns for both work and services after the construction of a limited-access high speed highway along the entire length of the valley. Linked to a four lane commuter highway to Halifax, it effectively renders the whole area more and more dependent on metropolitan Halifax, whose suburbs now creep relentlessly across the peninsula towards Windsor. At the same time, the new highway encourages growth of a number of commercial centres such as the service and retail strips near Kentville/New Minas.

8.   Margaret Conrad, "Apple Blossom Time in the Annapolis Valley, 1880–1957," in *The Acadiensis Reader: Volume II Atlantic Canada After Confederation* (second edition), P.A. Buckner and David Frank (eds.) (Fredericton, 1988).

The importance of military bases and universities to this agricultural zone cannot be overestimated. Decisions to locate and expand such institutions have been politically charged. Bureaucrats and university professionals contribute disproportionately to the economy of towns in these sub-regions, providing steady and relatively high earnings for large numbers of local residents, who service the consuming tendencies of students and faculty alike. A considerable amount of political manoeuvring has occurred to ensure the continued presence of these institutions in areas of relatively low population density, a subject of constant political concern in rural areas. The University of New Brunswick, located at Fredericton since its establishment in the eighteenth century, had to recognize Saint John's need for its own branch of the university and opened a second campus there in the 1970s. But there have been few such compromises to the historic identity of institutions with their smaller communities of origin.

Coastal Littorals

Throughout Atlantic Canada settlers situated at convenient spots along coastlines or natural waterways, which became commercial and service centres for their immediate sub-areas. Taken together they constitute an ill-defined hierarchy of resource-based communities. As roads, railways and highways supplemented water-based transport, these various systems became more integrated or were even

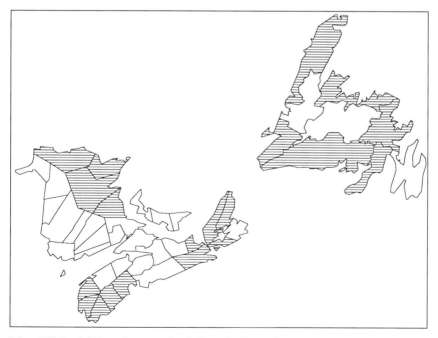

Map III.3   Littoral zones in Atlantic Canada

abandoned in some cases, as the rush to concentrate services took hold.

Until very recently, urban/rural profiles of census districts within littoral areas remained largely unaffected by those economic changes that propelled the region as a whole towards higher levels of urbanization. Government intervention has dramatically affected the nature of both urban and rural life along these margins since World War II, mostly through improvements in transportation and in the delivery of various services. Today, even the most remote settlements have access to such a wide variety of urban-based services that it is sometimes difficult to decide when rural life-styles leave off and integration with a larger community begins (see Map III.3).

Nova Scotia

Nova Scotia's Atlantic coast-line was settled during the closing decades of the eighteenth century by a mixture of Loyalists, Scots, and small numbers of returning Acadians and Black refugees and Loyalists.[9] With populations spread across a large expanse of territory, primarily dependent on fish as its staple, few towns of any significant size were needed. County shire towns benefitted from the somewhat accidental location of government institutions there. For instance, originally there was substantial farming in Antigonish, which was settled by large numbers of highland Scots. The presence of Roman Catholic diocesan offices and Saint Francis Xavier University, servicing the largely Roman Catholic population of the surrounding counties, effectively transformed a farming village into a fair-sized town, a process accelerated in the post-1960s period with expansion of the university and, through a process of political manoeuvring, the location there of a number of federal government offices.

Port Hawkesbury, on the Cape Breton side of Canso Straight, experienced a boom following construction of the Causeway in 1956. Construction of new highways designed to assist the location of industries actually facilitated creation of a number of shopping malls and motels on the outskirts of the town, a process assisted by interventions from both federal and provincial governments.[10] Another exception to the preponderance of fish, farm and forest related activities along these coasts occurred in the town of Inverness where, between 1903 and 1933, two large coal mines controlled by central Canadian capitalists led to a population explosion from 300 to almost 3000 people. The

---

9.   Included in the Nova Scotia littoral are the mainland counties of: Digby, Yarmouth, Shelburne, Queens, Lunenburg, Guysborough, Antigonish, and the three Cape Breton Counties of Inverness, Richmond, and Victoria.

10.   Foote, *The Case of Port Hawkesbury…*

boom was short-lived however, and the population subsequently fell to 2,000 when the mines closed during the depression. A more severe example of the same sort of arrested development occurred at nearby Mabou, where mining was even more short lived. Miscalculations regarding the size of the coal seam proved fatal to the continuance of the mine. Other incidents of this sort of investment followed by sharp

Mabou coal mines, ca 1905
One new industrial community disappeared following abandonment of its coal mine. Established during the rush for development after 1900, the mine was soon abandoned. The houses pictured here, remarkably like those provided by companies in other mining towns on Cape Breton, was moved following abandonment of the mine. *Source: Beaton Institute, University College of Cape Breton*

declines occurred everywhere, though they often required construction of large plants and company houses in rural areas.[11]

Along Nova Scotia's South Shore, the LaHave and Mersey Rivers serve as natural routes to rich timber and farming areas. The E.D. Davidson Company, established at Bridgewater in 1865, processed much of the timber sawn in the LaHave River valley. After steam power arrived at Bridgewater in 1890, carding and flour mills were established to process wool and wheat from the fertile farmlands of Lunenburg County. Further down shore, at Liverpool, lumber mills and later, the Bowaters pulp and paper mill processed the timber that was floated down the Mersey (see Fig. III.3).

Lunenburg town, known best for the boat-builders and yards that produced the famous *Bluenose* eclipsed smaller ports along the shore as a major fish-outfitting centre during the hey-day of the Grand Banks schooner fishery. The main resource serviced by Lunenburg, as well as

11. Danny Sampson, "The Making of a Cape Breton Coal Town: dependent development in Inverness, Nova Scotia, 1889–1915," M.A. Thesis, University of New Brunswick, 1988.

Figure III.3 Population growth of south shore towns, 1871–1991

(Thousands of persons)

- Digby
- Shelburne
- Lunenburg
- Liverpool
- Bridgewater
- Yarmouth

1871   1891   1911   1931   1951   1971   1991

the towns of Shelburne, Yarmouth and Digby, was and remains the fish caught in off-shore waters. Though Bridgewater and Yarmouth are now the primary commercial centres of the South Shore, smaller towns maintain their position through a local network of service and retail enterprises.

Yarmouth's shipping and ship-building industries, based on timber rafted from neighbouring communities, prospered throughout the nineteenth century. A major transformation occurred beginning in the 1880s, with establishment of a cotton mill, the expansion of an already large iron foundry and a number of smaller industries. But Yarmouth languished after 1900 and

Lunenburg boat building, ca 1910

Ship and boat-building were a common occurrence along the coasts. Even though it was the most wide-spread industrial activity in the region before 1900, little town development was associated with ship-building. Bays and sheltered coves provided sites for construction, not in factory setting, but in the open air, where materials and labour could be brought together for the assembly of the vessels. *Source: United Church of Canada Archives*

subsequently concentrated on its entrepôt or "Gateway" functions as the Nova Scotia port closest to the United States. Fresh fish leave the port and tourists enter the province through Yarmouth.[12]

Yarmouth Post Office, ca 1900
Throughout the region urbanization was accompanied by construction of new public buildings, often necessitated by sudden population growth. Many were built by the federal government, which responded to urban growth with a massive program of building post offices and customs houses. The style of such buildings was replicated in small towns across the Dominion. Yarmouth's was situated along a refurbished Main Street, which would host a number of other impressive buildings as well. *Source: Yarmouth County Historical Society and Museum.*

In eastern Nova Scotia and rural Cape Breton fishing, farming and pulp making are the primary activities. Port Hawkesbury and Antigonish are the only incorporated towns there, reflecting lower levels of urban development. In the nineteenth century the presence of Jersey Island-based fishing firms at Arichat on Isle Madame and in Cheticamp on Cape Breton's north coast set the trend for outside control over marketing resources to the outside. This trend was reinforced by the subsequent arrival to the area of large fish-packers controlled from Halifax. Subsequently, a cooperative movement emerged in the area, primarily directed toward rural production activities and did not generate substantial urban places. Since the 1950s a number of new fish processing plants have been established, but they are mostly a throwback to the older system with control maintained from outside. Today Port Hawkesbury depends on the Swedish-based STORA pulp mill, which trucks pulp logs to its plant from all across eastern Nova Scotia.

The outstanding demographic characteristic of this zone is its virtually flat population curve, for both urban and rural sectors. People have had difficulty finding opportunities to supplement subsistence-level farming and fishing. Hence, it has always been the area within the region with highest levels of out-migration. Even as new industries have been established throughout the zone in the post-1950s era, there has been little expansion of urban infra-structures. New

12. Muise, "The Industrial Context of Inequality…"

employers, such as STORA at Port Hawkesbury and the Michelin Tire
Plant at Bridgewater, while demanding urban services such as water
and electric power and a modern plant, (most of it provided by gener-
ous agreements with provincial and federal governments) do not
require substantial numbers of town-based workers. Instead, most
workers come to the huge plants from the surrounding rural communities, taking advantage of the new highways designed for movement
of pulp wood or for facilitating large numbers of tourists through the
area's burgeoning tourist industry, which is now the most intensely
developed industry along the region's littorals.

**Figure III.4   Urban/rural population change in Nova Scotia lit-
toral zone, 1871–1991**

(Thousands of persons)

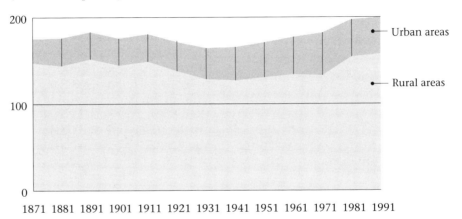

Towns: Digby, Yarmouth, Shelburne, Liverpool,
Lunenburg, Bridgewater, Canso, Antingonish,
Port Hawkesbury, Inverness, Cheticamp.

Consolidation of health and education services into a few larger
centres has been a dramatic by-product of improvements to the
transportation systems. Abandonment of virtually all the rail lines
throughout these littoral areas (throughout the entire region for that
matter) has meant increased dependence on the highway network for
both the shipment of staples and movement of people. Today, a considerable amount of every rural resident's time, particularly that of
school children, is taken up reaching services offered only in larger
centres. The tendency to consolidate ever more of these services as the
rural communities become even more thinly populated is not without
controversy as communities struggle to maintain the institutions that
are so central to their own identities.

New Brunswick

New Brunswick's north shore has experienced adverse economic and social conditions for a large part of its history.[13] Under-development there is characterized by a narrow dependency on staples exploitation, dominated by outside-based fish and timber companies. Historically this issue was further complicated by the fact that these externally-based companies were anglophone, while residents were mostly Acadians. A string of villages based on fishing, and a few larger forestry dominated centres, also provided specialized services for residents along the littoral. Campbellton, Dalhousie, Bathurst, Newcastle and Chatham all went through the same sequence of dependencies, with growth restricted by the demands of the successive staples processing industries established in each town at various times over the past century.[14]

In the post-1960s era, these towns have concentrated on delivering services to the surrounding communities and supplying the inputs needed by mining and pulp and paper-making industries located along the south shore of the Bay of Chaleur and at the mouth of the Miramichi River. Newcastle and Chatham, located only a few kilometres apart on opposite sides of the

Chatham, 1910
Like other early saw-mill and paper-making towns, Chatham's lumber mills were located along the waterfront where easy access to transportation facilities gave an immediacy to the settlement. Houses and businesses crowded around the older mills to allow easy access by foot to workers who, in a pre-automobile era, needed to live close by their places of employment. *Source: Provincial Archives of New Brunswick*

13. Restigouche, Northumberland, Kent and Gloucester counties are included in the New Brunswick littoral.
14. Rosemary Ommer, *From Outpost to Outport: A Structural Analysis of the Jersey-Gaspe Cod Fishery, 1786–1886* (Montreal/ Kingston, 1991); and Graeme Wynn, *Timber Colony: A Historical Geography of Early Nineteenth Century New Brunswick* (Toronto, 1981).

Miramichi River, were originally two distinct centres. But growth along their intervening boundaries has been so large that today it is difficult to establish their boundaries and a typical strip of urban services has emerged along the routes that join the two major towns. Newcastle, home to one of the oldest and largest pulp and paper mills in the region, continues the tradition of wood dependency established in the nineteenth century when the Miramichi was one of North America's premier lumbering rivers.

The Bathurst/Dalhousie/Campbellton area below is another instance of this process. Located along the south shore of the Bay of Chaleur, these communities served as lumbering and fishing centres with little urban infrastructure prior to Confederation. After arrival of steam-powered lumber mills and construction of the Intercolonial Railway (which passed through Campbellton in the 1870s), lumbering came to replace the older timber industry that had dominated the earlier era. In 1928, the International Paper Company set up a $20 million pulp mill at Dalhousie and demands for labour made it the resource processing and service centre for a predominantly Acadian area, a function which it shares with Bathurst, which emerged in the post 1950s period as the centre for the active mineral industry of the region.

The demographic trend of New Brunswick's north shore, unlike that of Nova Scotia's littorals, is distinguished by its steady population growth, almost triple its base of 60,000 in 1871. Part of this can be explained by the fecundity of a predominantly Acadian and Irish Roman Catholic population, who together make up the vast majority

Figure III.5   Urban/rural population change in New Brunswick littoral zone, 1871–1991

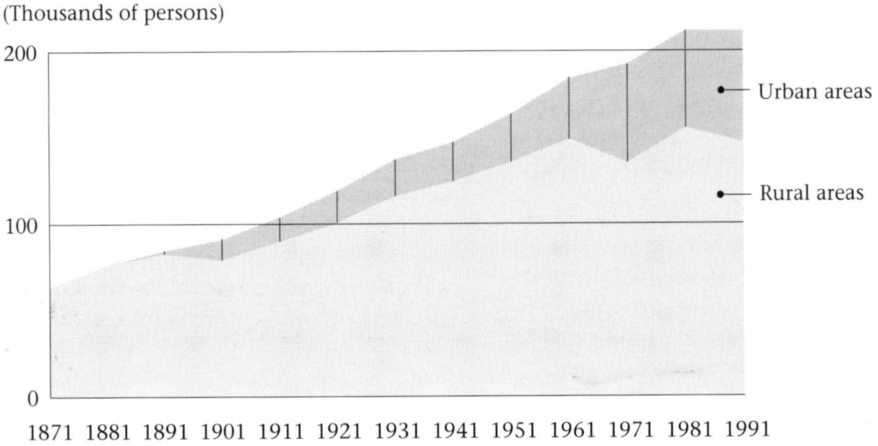

(Thousands of persons)

Towns: Bathurst, Campbellton, Chatham, Newcastle, Dalhousie.

of the people of this area. This has been compounded by New Brunswick Acadians' tendency to migrate less readily than their anglophone counterparts. The Acadian dominated Roman Catholic church

Belledune, New Brunswick, 1980

actively discouraged out-migration and promoted colonization, pressuring people to occupy homesteads in previously unoccupied rural areas[15] (see Fig. III.5).

    In the 1960s, with unemployment rates double national averages and with little hope of remedial action, the federal and provincial governments signed the first of a series of agreements under the Fund for Rural Economic Development (FRED). Communities were assisted in installing services deemed necessary to attract industries, and various government agencies urged rural residents to relocate to larger

One of the success stories of the modern economy has been the base-metal industry of northeastern New Brunswick. These ore refinery and processors represent a very high level technology, controlled by Brunswick Mining and Smelting, an American based corporation. These processors came to the area as a consequence of massive incentives offered by both provincial and federal governments, who supplied the roads, wharves, etc. needed to develop the area's resources. In the foreground of this photo is the large coal powered thermal generating plant of New Brunswick Power; the Brunswick Smelter is in the background. *Source: New Brunswick Information Services*

15. E.R. Forbes, "The 1930s...."

urban centres. These development programs were modified many times, making the area one of the great experiments in government-managed economic development in the post-1950s era.[16] At the same time, reforms initiated by the Louis J. Robichaud government, following the recommendations of the Byrne Commission, (headed not incidentally by a native of Bathurst) led to construction of a number of much needed schools and hospitals. As well, municipal reform enlarged town boundaries and increased populations in the major towns.

Figure III.6 Population change of northern New Brunswick towns, 1901–91

(Thousands of persons)

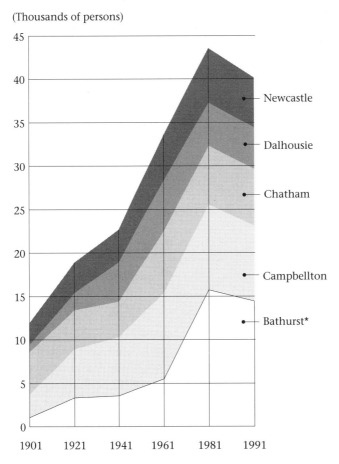

* Bathurst's dramatic increase following
  1961 is partially a result of extension
  of its boundaries.

16. Donald J. Savoie, *La lutte pour le développement: Le cas du Nord-Est* (Quebec, 1989), 49–50; and *Regional Economic Development: Canada's Search for Solutions* (Toronto, 1991).

Under DREE programs, communities linked to new resource processing centres, of which Bathurst is a good example, expanded rapidly. This resulted mainly from government investment in construction of better roads, which permitted residents all along the shore to commute to urban centres with relative ease. Urban/rural ratios that had remained relatively unchanged up to 1960, changed dramatically after the federal government concentrated its efforts on road construction and installation of services for industrial parks. The provincial government, for its part, aimed at attracting new businesses through tax and other incentives, including even the construction of factories or participation in their development. At Belledune, the federal government undertook construction of a wharf and approach roads, and the provincial government offered tax and other concessions for locating there, including a guarantee of the twenty million dollars necessary to build a smelter and chemical complex. The province also guaranteed expropriation rights, a ten year monopoly on smelting lead and zinc concentrates, and water rights and a long term tax holiday.[17]

Newfoundland

In Newfoundland, settlement spread north and south on either side of St. John's.[18] Outside the Avalon Peninsula, where over half of Newfoundlanders live today, only a few towns emerged. The nature of the inshore fishery was such that most people lived in smaller villages close by the migrating cod stocks that constituted the colony's primary staple.[19] As a consequence, little urbanization occurred until J.R. Smallwood's post-1949 government attempted to resettle residents into larger towns. The *Centralization Program*, begun in 1953, urged people to move out of communities that lacked health, education, and other facilities, to designated growth areas.

The *Newfoundland Resettlement Program,* which involved both the federal and provincial governments, was a more extensive version of

17. Della M.M. Stanley, *Louis Robichaud: A Decade of Power...;* Jim Kenny, "Getting the Lead Out: State Capital and Community Development of the New Brunswick Base Metal Industry, 1950-1975." Ph.D. Thesis, Carleton University (in progress).

18. Included in the Newfoundland littoral are census divisions 2 [Burin Peninsula]; 3 [Burgeo, Channel-Port aux Basques]; 4 [St. Georges]; 7 [Bonavista]; 8 [Baie Verte]; 9 [Northern Peninsula]. For much of Newfoundland's history Labrador was a thinly settled seasonal fishing zone. Major mining and hydro-electric development transformed its interior until today its population is urban and industrial; so is excluded from the littoral zone.

19. Shannon Ryan, *Fish Out of Water: The Newfoundland Saltfish Trade, 1814–1914* (St.John's, 1986); and David Alexander, *The Decay of Trade: The Newfoundland Salt-fish Trade, 1935–1965* (St.John's, 1976). The implications of these developments for the distribution of populations in Newfoundland has been a matter of constant debate among both social scientists and public policy-makers. See John J. Mannion (ed.), *The Peopling of Newfoundland: Essays in Historical Geography* (St. John's, 1977).

Two ways of processing fish
These two photos illustrate the
massive change occurring during
the past few decades. In the pre-
industrial era, men and women
prepared fish to allow nature to
take its course. Modern fish plants,
such as the one pictured here in
Lunenburg, requires a much more
concentrated work-force and large
doses of technology. One of the
consequences has been a much
higher level of urbanization in the
littoral areas of Newfoundland.
*Source: United Church of Canada
Archives and Nova Scotia Information Services*

the centralization program, and operated into the 1960s. Both these
schemes functioned in a similar manner: financial incentives were
offered to householders to move to growth centres identified by the
government. While many moved, the bulk of the Island's littoral
population remained rural. Attempts at community restructuring
such as these were heavy-handed efforts at social change. While the
Newfoundland case was a clear example of the bureaucratic arrogance,
it typified what was being attempted by various means across the
region during that period. The Newfoundland case is peculiar for the
extensiveness of the intervention and the absence of landward transportation systems linking smaller communities with one another. In
other parts of the region attempts have been more subtle, though the
commitment of local communities to defend their integrity has sometimes been as fierce and the consequences as grave.

The demographic profile of rural Newfoundland is much like that
of northern New Brunswick, the population almost tripled, from about
70,000 to about 200,000 over the past 125 years. The limited amount
of processing required for the saltfish trade placed a premium on spac-
ing communities wide apart for shore-based fishing. As a consequence,
very few of the urban services common elsewhere were developed; nor
was there much land-based transportation needed between communities. Since much of the profit from the cod trade flowed out of villages
toward the larger towns, or to St. John's, inadequate surplus value was
left behind to provide the tax base necessary for developing services.

A number of growth poles have emerged on Newfoundland's southern and eastern shores, around the major bays, while portions of the west and south coasts continue to be less densely populated. The east coast, where Northern Cod has proven to be the focal-point, has been threatened as never before by increased pressures brought on by a consolidation of capital involved in both catching and processing catches.

Predominantly rural zones, whether farming, fishing, or forestry centred, have undergone radical change over the past quarter century. The locally-based merchants and artisans of an earlier era have been supplemented in more recent times by networks of shopping malls and chain stores. State-supported institutions such as post-offices, secondary schools and hospitals, tend to be concentrated in larger villages and towns. With expansion of the welfare state, many smaller towns deliver social programs that were unavailable to rural dwellers before the modern era. The result has been a dramatic increase in the numbers of people who work in service sectors within towns participating in the process.

Wherever profits allow, farm and fish production has been tailored to suit large conglomerate food-processing companies. The Saint John River valley counties of Carleton and Victoria, where New Brunswick's potato production has become concentrated, is heavily influenced by the McCain food empire. The United Fruit Co-operative controls much of Nova Scotia's apple production. The Irving group, operating as Cavendish Farms, dominates a large amount of agricultural output on Prince Edward Island. These developments in agriculture parallel what is happening in fishing, though an amazing persistence of

Figure III.7   Urban/rural population change in Newfoundland littoral zone, 1874–1991

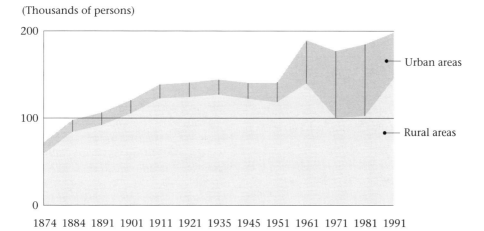

(Thousands of persons)

smaller forms of capitalism remain in place in many communities. In many villages, particularly in eastern Nova Scotia and New Brunswick as well as Prince Edward Island, both consumer and producer co-operatives and credit unions offer a counter-weight to the larger corporations.[20]

Michelin tire plant, Bridgewater, Nova Scotia

While each of these predominantly rural sub-districts has become more urbanized to some extent over the past twenty years, centres in all five zones have failed to exercise a complete monopoly on services. Essential services are delivered directly to rural people almost as efficiently as they are to towns and cities. While commercial activity has boomed in well established urban areas, services have become

This photo portrays the influence of industrial development on some rural areas. This tire plant, like many other modern factories and resource processing establishments, was located on unoccupied lands conveniently located for receiving and shipping materials. Its huge parking lot is one of the important indicators of the source of its workers most of whom come from a wide surrounding territory. *Source: Nova Scotia Information Services*

20.   Murphy, "From Family Farming to Capitalist Agriculture…"; Barratt and Apostle, *Emptying their Nets…;* and *Journal of Canadian Studies* 19, 1 (Spring, 1984).

available on the outskirts, where shopping malls have made their impact felt. Interestingly enough, improvements to highway systems in many cases contributes to the continuing rural character of these zones by permitting rural dwellers to have access to a full range of the sorts of goods and services that town dwellers take for granted.

In some circumstances, the more recent arrival of resource industries has had less of an impact than in any previous era. Improved roads permit rural residents to retain their rural lifestyle, yet commute to jobs in town. It has therefore become less necessary for workers to migrate permanently to higher-density centres. Resource-processors as well have been given access to the necessary raw materials, such as pulp logs, with the help of improved roadways.

These coastal and farming based towns have come to dominate sub-regions in ways inconceivable during an earlier era, when household self-sufficiency was more pronounced. Given limited access to local transportation, in the pre-automobile era, workers lived close to their places of employment, contributing directly to the urban boom of the *National Policy* era, even in smaller towns. The huge parking lots adjacent to post-industrial age factories testifies to their dependence on a mobile workforce, very few of whom actually live near their place of employment. These parking lots are paralleled by similar-sized lots at shopping malls, invariably located on the edge of existing towns where the new highways are designed to by-pass the older urban centres. The result has been little significant alteration of rural-urban ratios, except in northern New Brunswick and Newfoundland, where increased urban concentrations have been a produced by deliberate government intervention.

Chapter IV

Metropolises and Industrial Towns: Zones of Persistent Urbaneness

Two distinct urban-dominant areas have emerged in Atlantic Canada. Halifax, Saint John and St. John's, the three principal *Metropolitan Centres,* have large, high-density populations and perform service functions for a significant part of their surrounding territory as well as serving as centres of industry and commerce. The region's four *Industrial Zones* are centred on Sydney, New Glasgow and Moncton/ Amherst in the Maritimes; and on the Corner Brook/Grand Falls census districts in Newfoundland. While each has its own quite diverse social structure and historical experience, none have the depth or breadth of urban services displayed by the three metropolitan centres (see Map IV.1).[1]

Halifax, Saint John and St. John's have been persistently urban from their establishment in the eighteenth century. As capital of Nova Scotia Halifax has historically been military, administrative and commercial centre to the province. While it failed to dominate a provincial urban network for much of its history, today it serves as regional headquarters for financial, government, commercial and transportation/ communication services, most with their head offices in central Canada. Saint John, besides being an industrial centre based on lumber, manufacturing and oil refining, has traditionally performed entrepôt functions for the Saint John Valley. St. John's, is its province's dominant commercial centre as well as its political capital.

---

1.   Establishing the relationship of metro populations to their census districts can be problematic. Halifax County has a diverse rural population as well as the large city of Dartmouth, across the harbour but integrated with the city. Saint John has gradually expanded its city boundaries, until it is virtually co-terminus with the census district of Saint John County. St. John's is the largest community on the Avalon Peninsula. Some large suburban towns are attached to St. John's, but a number of other towns around the coasts of the Avalon peninsula contribute to the district's urban mixture.

The combined population of the three metro areas exceeds 600,000, an increase in their proportion of the region's population from under 10% in 1871 to over 25% today (see Fig. IV.1).

Halifax

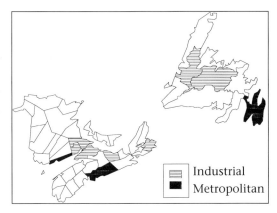

Map IV.1   Metropolitan and industrial zones

Halifax County stretches close to 200 kilometres along Nova Scotia's east coast, but extends back from the sea towards the province's spine for only about 30 kilometres at its widest point. It is Nova Scotia's largest county by area and population. A sprawling metro complex has evolved surrounding Halifax harbour, which now includes the city of Dartmouth, as well as the municipalities of Bedford and Sackville. The city itself had long suffered from the confines of its peninsular location, which inhibited expansion and made access

Figure IV.1   Population growth of metropolitan areas, 1871–1991

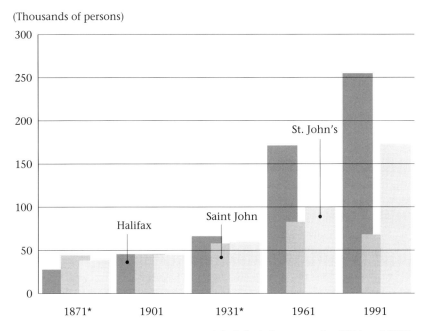

(Thousands of persons)

* St. John's figures are for 1874 and 1935.

to the city's central core from peripheral areas through the narrow neck of the peninsula difficult in periods of heavy traffic. For many common services, Halifax and Dartmouth, along with adjoining municipalities, now come under the jurisdiction of the Halifax and Dartmouth Metropolitan Authority, a system similar to arrangements for regional government in many of Canada's larger urban centres.

The eastern and western portions of the county, which lie outside the Metro Authority, include a number of rural communities dependent on inshore fishing and some marginal farming areas, which contain less than 10% of county population. Construction of high-speed trunk highways has enabled Metro to absorb outlying communities into its sphere of influence. Today, workers from towns as far away as Lunenburg to the south and Windsor and Truro to the west commute to Halifax for work.

Halifax has become the shopping and entertainment centre for Nova Scotia, with a series of festivals and various sporting and entertainment spectacles following one after the another all year round. Shoppers come from distant communities, for there are more retail outlets in Metro than anywhere else in the Atlantic region. Other attractions designed to attract tourists from near and far include a refurbished downtown, a development undertaken at enormous public expense, which is anchored by the Scotia Square Project. A dramatic transformation of the down town includes a rebuilt waterfront area designed for sightseers and festival shoppers.

Throughout the nineteenth century, Halifax, as the principal merchant shipping port of Nova Scotia, had as well enjoyed primacy as a military and bureaucratic centre as well. Its social and economic activities were driven by some of the wealthiest merchants in the region.[2] In the twenty years surrounding Confederation, Halifax developed from a colonial town of just 15,000 to a city of 30,000. Over the next half century, its was relatively unaffected by the industrial surge that influenced other towns in the province. Its population rose sharply between 1911 and 1921, mostly due to war-related activity, when the city grew beyond the capacity of available housing, a situation worsened by the massive explosion that levelled much of the north end's working class neighbourhoods in 1917[2] (see Fig. IV.2).

Population growth flattened out in the 1920s when times were hard and out-migration from the Atlantic region peaked. But beginning in the later 1930s, Halifax County's urban population began a steady climb. During World War II, as Halifax once again became a

2.   Judith Fingard, "Masters and Friends, Crimps and Abstainers: Agents of Control in 19th Century Sailortown," in *Acadiensis* VIII, 1 (Autumn 1978); and Judith Fingard, *The Dark Side of Life in Victorian Halifax* (Porter's Lake, 1989).

Figure IV.2 Urban/rural population change in Halifax County, 1871–1991

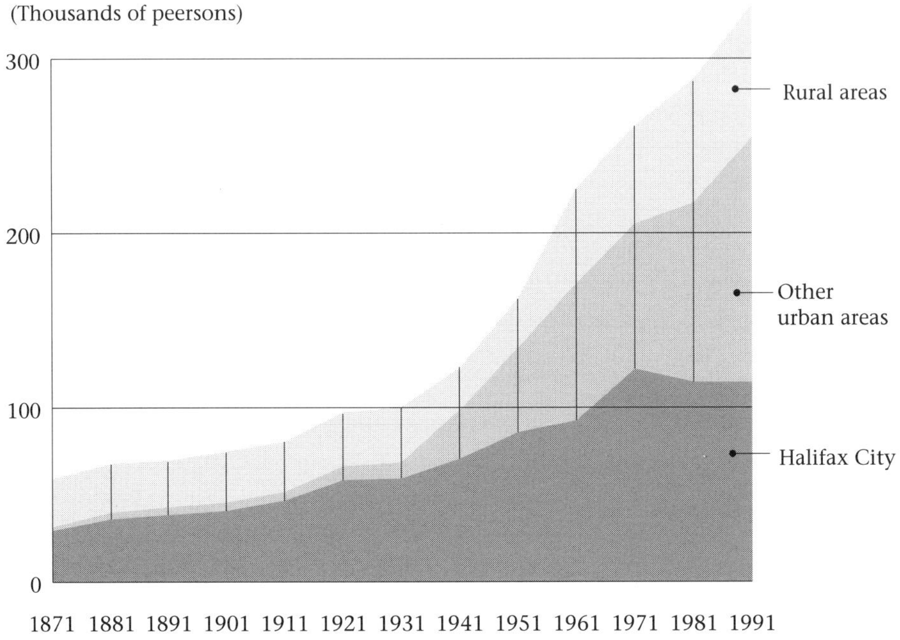

(Thousands of peersons)

Major towns include Halifax and Dartmouth.

focal point for launching Canada's war effort in Europe and in the North Atlantic, the city's population grew by 20%. Across the harbour, Dartmouth grew by 50%. The fringe (an area within a 10-kilometre radius of Halifax/Dartmouth) population, grew by over 40%. After the war, this fringe area was separated from the rural municipality of Halifax County and gradually integrated into the city's planning structure.[3]

The scarcity of real estate on Halifax's main peninsula was over-come by transit improvements that allowed large numbers of com-muters to flood into the city from surrounding communities on a daily basis. Important to that scheme were two harbour bridges, one built in the mid-1950s and the other 15 years later in the early 1970s, which further integrated Dartmouth and Halifax. Since 1971, the population

3. L.D. McCann, "Staples and the New Industrialism …"; and "Port Development in Halifax," [Plate 25] in *Historical Atlas of Canada…*; John C. Weaver, "Reconstruction of the Richmond District of Halifax: A Canadian Episode in Public Housing and Town Planning, 1918–1921," in *Plan Canada* 16,1 (March, 1976); Suzanne Morton, "The Halifax Relief Commission and Labour Relations during the Reconstruction of Halifax, 1917–1919," in *Acadiensis* XVIII, 2 (Spring, 1989); and John Bacher, "From Study to Reality: The Establishment of Public Housing in Halifax, 1930–1953," in *Acadiensis* XVIII,1 (Autumn, 1988).

of Halifax has been in decline, but other urban areas, along with the rural fringe continue to grow.

In 1956 the Stephenson Report, commissioned by the Nova Scotia government, provided a rationale for urban renewal and downtown redevelopment. Included in its recommendations was a proposal for the elimination of the Black community of Africville; a group of eighty

or so households situated just to the north of the dock-yards where the harbour opened into Bedford Basin.[4] Africville, even though it was home to a well-developed community, had never been supplied with urban services such as water and sewerage. The bureaucratic urban planning bulldozer levelled existing communities with little concern for the inhabitants historical patterns of settlement or long-range planning. The result was further displacement of residents away from the city. The second harbour bridge,

The Hydrostone subdivision, Halifax, 1930
The Halifax explosion of 1917 levelled much of the north end of the city. It provided one of the important occasions for community development in the history of the region. This aerial, showing the Hydrostone on the right reveals the homogeneity involved in Thomas Adams' plan for an integrated community utilizing many British norms for street lay-out and building styles etc. The less planned neighbourhoods to the left were more typical of the less regulated developments of the pre-explosion era. *Source: Public Archives of Nova Scotia.*

4.   R.G. Speller, "The Halifax Metropolitan Area, 1947," in *Reorganization of Provincial-Municipal Relations in Nova Scotia*, D.C. Rowat (ed.) (Halifax, 1949).

now rises high above the site and its approaches occupy part of the expropriated land.[5]

To the white middle class leadership of Halifax, the levelling of Africville was to be the dawn of improved race relations; to blacks, it became a symbol for activism against the racism so deeply imbedded within the established white community.[6] Yet, Africville represented just 10% of all Haligonians who were displaced by so called urban renewal projects during this era. At the height of the exodus, upwards of 200 families per month were being relocated to outlying areas of the city or into various public housing schemes in Halifax and Dartmouth. During the same time period between 10,000 and 15,000 people were relocated in Saint John as a result of similar redevelopment schemes[7] (see Map IV.2).

The Halifax waterfront, 1978
The impact of Halifax's progress as the business centre of the region is reflected in the sky-line of its central business district, which towers above the harbour and dwarfs the older nineteenth century buildings and wharves. In the background is the Angus L. MacDonald Bridge, linking the downtown with Dartmouth, on the other side of the harbour. *Source: Public Archives of Nova Scotia.*

Since World War II, there have been many changes in the economic base of metropolitan Halifax. Its labour force has almost quadrupled, from 43,209 in 1941 to 160,760 in 1986, though an increasing portion of those who work within Halifax and Dartmouth today live outside its boundaries. Manufacturing, which never played a large part in the economy of Halifax, is clearly on the decline. Also notable is the steady decline in the numbers employed in public administration and defense, a traditional function of the city. The city's emerging role as a service and entertainment centre to the entire Atlantic region is clearly evident in the tremendous growth in the community, business and personal service sectors, up from 7% in 1951 to a hefty 34% in 1986. One consequence of this function has been the

5.   D.C. Rowat, *Halifax: A Case for a Metropolitan Authority* (Halifax, 1949); Gordon Stephenson, *A Redevelopment Study of Halifax, Nova Scotia* (Halifax, 1957).
6.   Africville Genealogical Society, *Africville Remembered* (Halifax, 1992).
7.   Donald H. Clairmont and Dennis William Magill, *Africville: the Life and Death of a Canadian Black Community* (Toronto, 1987). For Saint John, see David Boucher, "Metropolitan Development…"

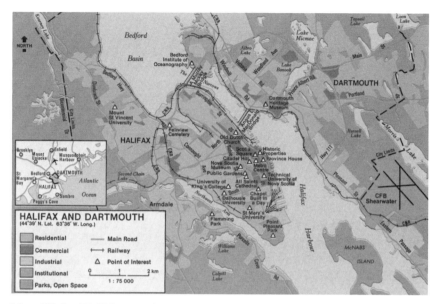

Map IV.2   Halifax and Dartmouth Urban Area

tremendous concentration of post-secondary education and specialized health resources in Halifax. Four major universities and a number
of colleges offer a wide variety of educational services. The region's

Figure IV.3   Sectors of Employment: Halifax, 1951–86

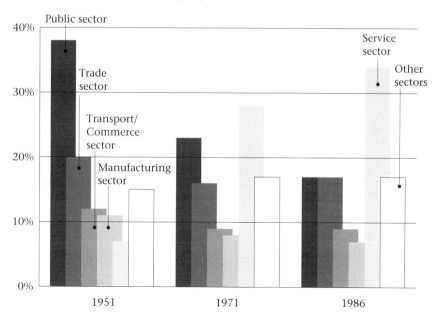

Figures calculated from Census Canada tables.

largest hospitals and university complex serve as both medical and educational centres for specialized health care and advanced education for people from throughout the region.[8]

Saint John

In the mid-nineteenth century, Saint John controlled the largest economic hinterland of any city in the region. Its early prosperity was based on the timber and shipbuilding economy of the "Wood, Wind and Sail" era. At Confederation, though a major city by British North American standards, Saint John was physically confined to a small peninsula backing on *Market Slip,* focal point of much of the city's Central Business District. The Carleton waterfront, on the west side of the harbour, contained the shipping terminals, saw mills and lumber yards upon which most of the city's prosperity was based.[9] Unlike Halifax, the city had large industrial suburbs both in the city proper and across and above the harbour itself, at Carleton and Portland, suburbs which it would soon absorb into its municipal borders.

Saint John County stretches along the Fundy shore in a narrow band. It contained a number of small towns with populations well under 1,000, most located well outside the city. St. Martins, to the east of the port, had established ship and lumber yards which were linked to Saint John's shipbuilding industry. Lancaster, to the west along a bend in the river, was the centre of a rich farming area that supplied garden produce to the city in its early days.[10]

Saint John's port was modernized after the fire of 1878 and, by 1890, the Canadian Pacific Railway completed its short line to terminals on the Carleton waterfront. Beginning in the 1880s, Saint John's business and political leaders linked their city's future to its functioning as a winter port for Canadian staples, shifting its main export commodity from lumber to grain. This change in function had a profound effect upon the city's working classes, as export of lumber in summer was slowly replaced by the export of grain during winter. As the peak labour period shifted, workers had also to deal with steamship companies head-quartered outside of Saint John instead of with the locally-based merchants who had previously controlled the docks. The complete transfer of harbour management from local to federal control would come in 1927, a result of the Royal Commission on Maritime Disabilities within Confederation.[11]

---

8.   For a perspective on employment distributions in the city towards the turn of the century, see L.D. McCann, "Port Development in Halifax…"

9.   T.W. Acheson, *Saint John: The Making of a Colonial Urban Community…*; Elizabeth McGahan, *The Port of Saint John…*

10.   Gregg Finley, "The Morans of St. Martins…," in *The Enterprising Canadians…,* Fischer and Sager (eds.).

Saint John's population curve is flatter than those of other metropolitan centres in the region, trailing off dramatically in the contemporary period. But after 1900, harbour activity increased and the city's population grew steadily. As with Halifax, two world wars provided economic stimulus, especially impacting

Saint John waterfront, c.1910
The very high tides on the Bay of Fundy had a unique impact on development of the historic waterfront in Saint John. Merchants were able to build elaborate wharves with their storehouses and outlets adjacent to the slips where their ships could dock. *Source: United Church of Canada Archives.*

the city's steel ship-building industry, which is today the most important in the region. By the 1920s, development of the Courtenay Bay area, east of the main peninsula, had transformed the harbour, giving it two major centres of activity. With the Saint John Drydock Company at the mouth of the Bay and new breakwaters protecting the approaches, harbour capacity was effectively doubled (see Fig. IV.4).

Since World War II the city has accommodated a variety of manufacturing enterprises, many controlled by the giant Irving conglomerate, which oversees much of the economic activity of the province. In Saint John, these include an oil refinery, a pulp mill, dry-dock and shipbuilding facilities, and a host of communication industries and real-estate development in the suburbs as well.[12] The dramatic increase

---

11. McGahan, *The Port of Saint John...*; on industrial transformation, see Robert Babcock, "The Saint John Street Railwaymen's Strike and Riot, 1914," in *Acadiensis* XI,2 (Spring, 1982).
12. John DeMont, *Citizens Irving: K.C. Irving and His Legacy* (Toronto 1991).

Figure IV.4   Urban/rural population change in Saint John County, 1871–1991

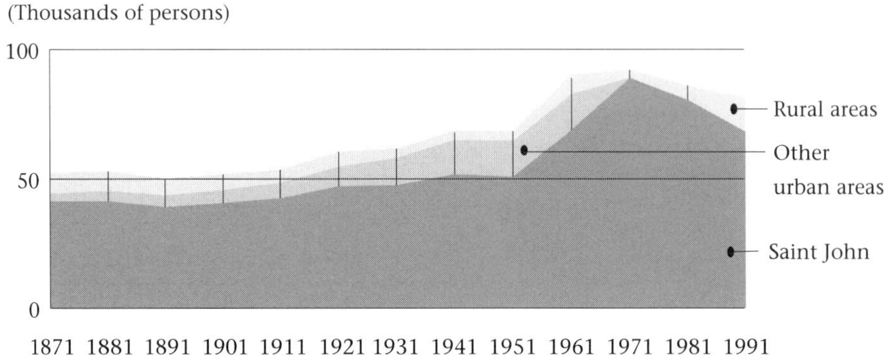

(Thousands of persons)

of Saint John County's population since World War II has been followed by steady decline since 1971, the latter to a large extent a function of the spread of suburbs north into neighbouring Kings County, where towns such as Rothesay and Quispamis have absorbed much of the suburban Saint John's new population centres.

Like Halifax, the older urban core has become depopulated, as people seek the outskirts where developers have assembled land for development of both housing and commercial outlets. At the same time the inner city has experienced major redevelopment. The modern highway system permits people who live in the more distant suburbs along the Kennebecasis River, to commute to jobs and services still concentrated in the city. Development of suburban housing and shopping malls has proceeded apace in Saint John as everywhere in the region, with similar implications for the central business district.

Many of the outlying villages were absorbed into the city in 1967 after the 1963 *Goldenberg Commission* recommended that Saint John's municipal boundaries be extended to include Simonds and Lancaster parishes. The extension gave the city a total area of 104 square miles, by far the largest city by area in the region and one of five largest in Canada. The remaining towns and villages, primarily in Kings County, are linked to Saint John through the census definition of the Metropolitan Area. They remain hesitant to come under Saint John's municipal jurisdiction after viewing the extent to which the city failed to live up to its commitments to Simonds and Lancaster after the 1967 amalgamation.[13]

The city's physical face was transformed in the 1970s with construction of a high-speed highway *The Throughway* cutting across the northern fringe of the older city, a new harbour bridge linked to the

13.   Boucher, "Metropolitan Development…"

throughway and new port facilities, and a number of downtown office and commercial complexes. A redevelopment scheme designed to highlight the older architecture of some of the old waterfront has cen-tred on Market Square where, again much like Halifax, festivals and celebrations are featured as tourist attractions. Loyalist Days have pro-vided a focal point for such development since the successful celebra-tion of the bicentennial of the Loyalist's 1784 landing in 1984.

Since the 1950s, Saint John's manufacturing sector, like Halifax, has become relatively less important as a component of the labour force. As in Halifax, the greatest increase in the labour force has been in the service sector.

Figure IV.5   Sectors of Employment: Saint John, 1951–86

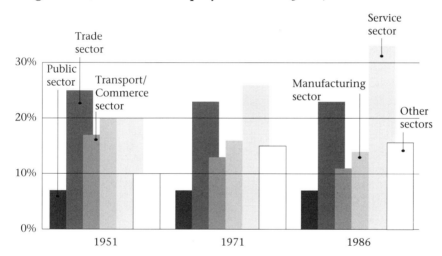

Figures calculated from Census Canada tables.

St. John's

St. John's has always asserted its dominance over the hundreds of out-ports strung out along Newfoundland's south and east coasts. Tradi-tionally, the city functioned as an outfitter and marketing entrepôt for fish and seal harvesters. The wealthiest and most powerful town in the colony, it also served as provincial capital, though it never developed the levels of government services, nor the growth pattern, of Halifax or Saint John.[14]

14. Paul O'Neill, *Seaport Legacy: The Story of St. John's, Nfld.* (Erin, 1976); Melvin Baker, "The Government of St. John's, Newfoundland: 1880–1921," Ph.D. Thesis, Univer-sity of Western Ontario, 1981; Baker, "Municipal Politics and Public Housing in St. John's, 1911–1921," in *Workingmen's St. John's*, Melvin Baker, Robert Cuff and William Earle Gillespie (eds.) (St. John's, 1982).

With little industry, save for those activities associated with fishing, there were few incentives for public works and much port activity continued to be controlled by merchants until quite recently. Their private wharves were both warehouses and outfitting stations for the schooners that plied the coastlines to gather the fish harvested and processed by outport fishermen. Most attempts at diversifying the local economy during the immediate post-1949 decade ended in failure, as the new provincial government tried to emulate the sorts of developmental decisions that were being attempted elsewhere. Since 1949, major changes have occurred to St. John's traditional role as the city evolved to provide a broader range of services to both local and international fishing fleets. More recently, the Hibernia off-shore oil project has raised hope for economic diversification and development once again.

From the mid-nineteenth century, economic diversification had been pursued by successive Newfoundland governments as the only alternative to the high levels of out-migration from rural areas of the colony. But, even after construction of a Newfoundland Railway during the closing decades of the century, little in the way of new enterprise occurred. With the twentieth century, a weakened and now thoroughly indebted provincial economy brought even more stagnation from both an economic and population perspective. The city, as the

Figure IV.6.   Urban/rural population change in Avalon Peninsula, 1874–1991

(Thousands of persons)

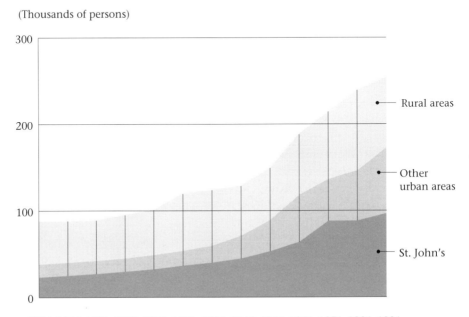

1874 1884 1891 1901 1911 1921 1935 1945 1951 1961 1971 1981 1991

financial and corporate centre of the old Dominion, was forced to deal with the ravages of unemployment and social dislocation without having any significant taxation base and very few of the amenities available in other communities of its size.

Determining metropolitan St. John's actual size can be problematic, particularly for the period before 1949 when there were so few municipal institutions in Newfoundland. Prior to 1949, little growth had occurred and out-lying communities remained unconnected to the capital by effective roads, though there was a very active coastal trade that was centred on the capital. Between 1951 and 1971, the metropolitan area population expanded from 52,873 to 88,102, followed by stagnation, much like that of Halifax and Saint John. As with the other communities, this is attributable to the growth of more distant residential suburbs such as Mount Pearl, which, though outside the city limits, is fully integrated in the metropolitan area.

In recent years, St. John's employment patterns shows trends similar to that of Halifax and Saint John as well. As with the other two, the most noticeable increase has been in the business/personal service category. Also of note is the virtual elimination of those employed in any sort of manufacturing. In St. John's, there has been, as well, a conspicuous drop in the relative importance of the transportation/communications/public utilities and the trade/commerce sectors.

Figure IV.7   Sectors of Employment: St. John's, 1951–86

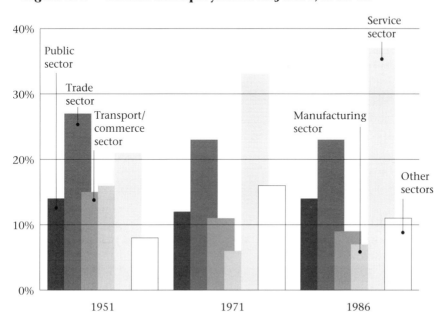

Figures calculated from Census Canada tables.

These three metropolitan centres share a number of features, both in their historical experience and their present condition. Most important recently has been the emergence of a ring of suburbs and satellite towns tied directly to the larger cities for the myriad of functions and services that form part of urban life today. This has been necessitated by the limited amount of land available in the core areas of all three cities, where relationships between available land and the waterfronts has been a defining force, both in the initial lay-out and subsequent development of their central business districts. Halifax and Saint John have natural geographic barriers to overcome in order to grow and expand. This has been eased somewhat by development of major transportation systems, bridges, roads and ferries, that permit the movement of larger numbers of people into and out of the urban core.

In the process of modernization, these cities have come to resemble those in other parts in Canada and North America. Large high-rise buildings, with their acres of apartments, hospital beds and office space, now dominate the skyline and overshadow the more traditional buildings during the period of initial expansion in the late nineteenth century. By and large, their redeveloped central business districts now focus upon recreation and tourism, providing a partial replacement for the flight of commercial establishments from the core to the shopping malls which ring all three cities and serve the suburbs, as well as the city proper.

The implications of these developments for the future of these communities has yet to be fully felt, though real-estate speculation in all three cities during the 1980s has produced a building boom that has increased the capacity of office and commercial space beyond immediate needs, leaving a residue of doubt concerning the future direction of development. Still, all three centres continue to attract large numbers of workers to their metro areas from the rest of the region, mostly because opportunities for employment there are still much better than in other places in the region.

Industrial Centres

An industrial zone, based on coal mining, steel-making and railway development, emerged between Sydney and Moncton. National Policy tariffs on imported coal and steel prompted industrial growth and urbanization in Nova Scotia's Pictou, Cape Breton and Cumberland counties, where iron foundries and steel plants were established to take advantage of nearby coal supplies. A fourth urban-industrial zone emerged only later with development of the pulp and paper industry in central Newfoundland. Developments in Nova Scotia and New Brunswick were part of a broad transformation of the regional economy that brought with it a massive movement of people into the urban zones.[15] Coal output increased every year until 1913, when it peaked at just over seven million tons. By that time, well over half of the coal produced in Nova Scotia was being used in steel-making, and related manufacturing industries in the region.

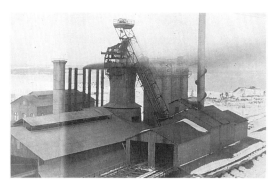

Scotia Steel blast furnace, Sydney Mines 1903
The Nova Scotia Steel and Coal Corporation built this plant to supply its Pictou county mills with the raw steel required to fabricate a wide range of manufactured products. It's coke ovens, blast furnace and open hearths, entirely American in design, were installed by Pennsylvania crews sent to ensure the new technology worked as per order. *Source: Public Archives of Nova Scotia.*

Construction of the Intercolonial Railroad was integral to this industrial transformation. As with most centres reliant on manufacturing for growth, towns in this area boomed and declined in response to general economic and market conditions. Centres which also served as agricultural service centres, railway hubs or which processed fish, experienced less severe population changes than those based solely on coal and steel.

Between 1900 and 1920 investments in manufacturing increased four-fold to $148.3 million in Nova Scotia; and five-fold, to $109 million in New Brunswick. These figures do not include the millions of dollars invested in new coal mining and lumbering operations during that period, both of which were tied directly to expansion of manufacturing. Regional manufacturers, operating a quite diverse industrial base, served both local and national markets. Amherst's Robb Engineering, for instance, made steam engines, boilers and water pumps, which were used across the country and achieved a global reputation for excellence. Moncton hosted a number of new industries, which included a sugar refinery and a cotton mill. It served as regional headquarters of the Intercolonial Railway and supported this role with a number of foundries and machine shops. Sydney's massive new steel complex was heralded as the most advanced in the world at the time of its construction in 1900.[16]

15. Acheson, "The National Policy and the Industrialization…"
16. The literature on industrialization is quite broad. For Moncton, see Daniel Hickey, "Moncton, 1871–1913: Le Commerce et l'industrie dans un carrefour ferroviaire,"

Social stratification deepened with industrialization and its atten-
dant population increases. As working class neighbourhoods became a
feature of industrial towns, the connection between where one lived
and where one worked became significant. New factories and railways
often divided neighbourhoods based on ethnicity and class. In
Amherst, for instance, the railway's yards separated the factories and
working-class subdivisions from the homes of the wealthy, as well as
from the older downtown commercial core. In mining communities,
companies built housing close to mine sites, so that miners would
have access to their work on foot. This practice was also followed in a
number of other industrial towns, where developers were anxious to
attract and retain skilled workers. In Cape Breton's coal towns, rapid
population growth resulted in crowded living conditions until company housing was constructed. The uniformity thus created was only
changed over a generation of development, after the company sold its
houses to their occupants. This initial housing stock, sometimes built
in haste, but with a degree of planning, still makes up the bulk of the
accommodation for workers in these towns.

Westmorland/Albert And Cumberland Counties[17]

Most urban growth in Westmorland, Albert and Cumberland counties
has occurred in Moncton, today one of the region's most dynamic
cities, and the second largest urban centre in New Brunswick. Located
at a bend of the Petitcodiac River near the high point of navigation, it
centres on agriculturally rich Westmorland County. In 1857, when the
first section of the European and North American Railway between
Shediac and Moncton was opened, Moncton was an important shipbuilding and shipping centre. The arrival of the railway, which would
soon be pushed westward to Saint John, signalled the town's transformation into an leading urban centre, a status confirmed in 1876,
when it became regional headquarters of the newly built Intercolonial
Railway.

With large railway repair shops dominating its industrial landscape, the town soon attracted a number of other industries. By 1920
it harboured over twenty-five different industrial establishments. Creation of new businesses, both large and small, continued through the

---

in *Moncton, 1871–1929: Changements socio-économiques dans une ville ferroviaire* ,
Daniel Hickey (ed.) (Moncton, 1990); Phyllis Leblanc, "Moncton, 1870–1937: A
Community in Transition," Ph.D. Thesis, University of Ottawa, 1988.

17.   Albert County is included along with Cumberland and Westmorland in this section, not because of any inherent urban qualities, but because, in the post-World
War II period, over half of its rather small population lives in Riverview, a suburb of
Moncton. The county's overall population was so small that its inclusion in the
pre-urban phase of its history does not distort urban/rural balances for the district.

1960s, by which time it had also developed into a prime distribution centre of central Canadian goods for the Maritimes. Recent growth in Moncton has been based on its service and administration sectors, the latter largely due to the presence there of a number of federal government offices. This occurred at the expense of an extension of its industrial base.

Even now its population continues to grow, though today its expansion is northward to meet the Trans-Canada highway by-pass, but becomes something of a road to new development. The Petitcodiac river, which serves as the boundary between Westmorland and Albert counties, also separates the neighbouring town of Riverview Heights from Moncton proper. Riverview, along with Dieppe, which lies just east of Moncton, has become fully integrated with the larger centre by an effective system of bridges and, more recently, by over-arching urban authorities that plan the infrastructure and other requirements for the entire area. Dieppe and Riverview heights have populations in excess of 10,000 each, but are functionally suburbs of Moncton.

Other urban centres in Westmorland are less directly tied to Moncton. Shediac, located on the Gulf of St. Lawrence shore and linked to Moncton by a modern highway, is the headquarters for a vibrant local fishery and is a major summer tourist destination. Sackville, known now as the location of Mount Alison University, lies between Moncton and Amherst along the Trans-Canada Highway. Today, it is primarily a

Figure IV.8   Urban/rural population change in Westmorland/ Albert and Cumberland Counties, 1871–1991

(Thousands of persons)

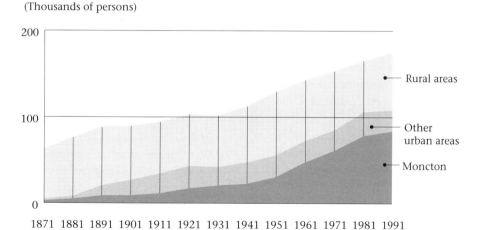

Towns: Moncton (including Dieppe and Riverview after 1961), Amherst, Springhill, Sackville and Shediac.

university town and still, to some extent, a service town for surrounding farms on the Tantramar marshes. But it was an industrial town of some consequence from late in the nineteenth century up to the 1950s, when its large foundry and stove factory were finally closed down.

In spite of the provincial boundary Nova Scotia's Cumberland County is functionally more linked to Moncton than to towns in Nova Scotia. The industrial town of Amherst and the coal mining town of Springhill are its major urban centres. Both have been relatively static since the 1920s. Amherst, like Moncton, had started out as the service centre for a prosperous agricultural and lumbering region. Following the 1870s, it profited from its location on the Intercolonial Railway and proximity to the coal fields of nearby Springhill, developed a number of successful factories. It achieved maximum industrial performance in the early 1900s and plunged into decline following World War I. It recovered temporarily during World War II, when its industrial sites were revived for war-time production, but its industrial employment would never equal that of its hey-day. Coal mining started at Springhill in the 1870s and continued until major mining disasters in 1956 and 1958 led to closure of its coal mines. Without any stable economic base the town's population, which peaked in 1941 at 7,170, has declined in recent years.[18]

Cape Breton County

Industrialization had a more profound effect on Cape Breton County than anywhere else the region. The county's urban population is contained within a 35-kilometre crescent of towns north and south of Sydney harbour. Sydney, Glace Bay, Sydney Mines, New Waterford, North Sydney, Dominion, Reserve and Louisbourg were all incorporated before World War I. Louisbourg is the only one outside the immediate industrial zone, though it too became tied to the industrial process when, for a number of years, its ice-free harbour served as the major coal shipping point during winter.

Between 1891 and 1901, the population of Cape Breton County's urban centres had doubled in size, from 18,611 to 39,841. Sydney alone increased from 2,427 to 9,909. The following decade Sydney's population almost redoubled; Glace Bay, home to eleven Dominion Coal Company collieries at one time or another, grew from 6,945 to 16,565. This super-heated growth was followed by stagnation and eventual decline.

18. Nolan Reilly, "The Emergence of Class Consciousness in Industrial Nova Scotia: A Case Study of Amherst, 1891–1925," Ph.D. Thesis, Dalhousie University, 1982; and Ian McKay, "Industry Work and Community in the Cumberland Coal Fields, 1848–1927," Ph.D. Thesis, Dalhousie University, 1983.

The urban proportion of Cape Breton County's population peaked at 86% of the total in 1931. Most towns continued to grow marginally until the 1960s, although relative levels of urbanization tumbled in the post-War era. In that era, towns experienced massive out-migration as both the coal and steel industries began their decline. In 1941, just 75% of the county population was urban. Today the urban percentage remains close to this figure, though the over-all population of the county, continues to

Parade at Senator's Corner, Glace Bay, c.1910
Towns became centres for celebration as well as work. This photo also illustrates the rapid acquisition of layers of technologies associated with the large concentrations of workers during a decade when Glace Bay was one of the fast growing communities in the region. The electric arc lights, street railways and stores and services typified the pre-automobile towns of the early twentieth century. *Source: United Church of Canada Archives.*

decline. Although the county's urban component is declining, an urban fringe outside the incorporated towns is fully integrated with the urban complex, and virtually the entire county is serviced by the intricate road system. A regional government [JOINTEX] looks after common services for the entire county, much as in other urban complexes throughout the region[19] (see Fig. IV.9).

19. Del Muise, "The Making of an Industrial Community: Cape Breton Coal Towns, 1867–1900," in *Cape Breton Historical Essays,* Don MacGillivray and Brian Tennyson (eds.) (Sydney, 1980); Ian McKay, "The Crisis of Dependant Development: Class

Figure IV.9   Urban/rural population change in Cape Breton County, 1871–1991

(Thousands of persons)

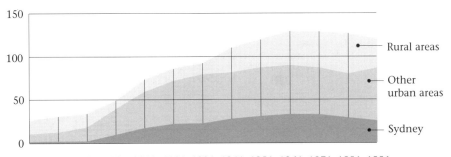

Towns: Sydney, Glace Bay, New Waterford, North Sydney, Sydney Mines.

Post-1921 population figures reflect the troubled times encountered by coal and steel in the post World War I era. The initial expansion of the steel and coal complex was linked directly to expansion of the Canadian economy, particularly to the high demand for steel rails as the country's northern and western frontiers were opened to exploitation. But Cape Breton's coal and steel failed to adjust to the more mature national economy of the post-World War I era. In 1921, the steel mill at Sydney Mines erected in 1903 by the Nova Scotia Steel Corporation closed permanently, a victim of industrial consolidation undertaken by the Montreal-based owners of the newly established British Empire Steel and Coal Corporation. This effectively emasculated the old Nova Scotia Coal and Steel Corporation.[20]

In attempting to extract extra profits from its Cape Breton coal and steel operations by reducing miners and steel workers wages, BESCO provoked the worst labour strife ever seen in the region. When its owners refused to invest in the technological improvements necessary to ensure continued viability of coal and steel, Cape Breton's industrial decline was assured. By the end of the 1920s, Cape Breton County had become a social and economic backwater of the Dominion economy, to be administered as a social problem, rather than integrated with a national economy.[21]

Conflict in the Nova Scotia Coalfields, 1872–1876," in *Class, Gender and Region: Essays in Canadian Historical Sociology*, Gregory S. Kealey (ed.)(St. John's, 1988); and Ron Crawley, "Class Conflict and the Establishment of the Sydney Steel Industry, 1897–1904," in *The Island: New Perspectives on Cape Breton's History, 1713–1990*, Kenneth Donovan (ed.) (Fredericton, 1989).

20. David Frank, "The Cape Breton Coal Industry and the Rise and Fall of the British Empire Steel Corporation," in *Acadiensis* VII, 1 (Autumn, 1977); and Sandberg, "Dependent Development…"

In Cape Breton, with the heaviest concentration of industrial workers east of Montreal, relations between a central Canada based corporation and its workers were intense and complicated. The deferential attitude of working-class citizens which allowed company officials to dominate municipal offices faded fast after the war. In consequence, there was substantial representation by working men on various town councils. In Sydney Mines, Glace Bay and New Waterford, this brought a more aggressive assessment of coal company assets for municipal tax purposes and a less submissive attitude during periods of labour conflict. Those towns, like others of the region, incurred substantial debts to finance infrastructures during their expansive years. Who should be responsible for providing services like water and electric power remained unsettled. Some municipalities left services in the hands of the coal company, causing serious problems during the industrial disputes of the 1920s and a series of difficult problems in the post 1930s period as towns had to take over the responsibility for providing services.[22]

The more recent history of coal and steel in Cape Breton is a litany of capital abandonment. Federal and provincial governments have both intervened in attempts to renew development or arrest decline. Dominion Coal had closed down most of its collieries in Glace Bay and New Waterford before it finally pulled out in 1967. Its operations were taken over by a federal crown corporation, the Cape Breton Development Corporation (DEVCO) which continued to reduce capacity of the industry by closing down older mines. A few more modern mines were established as well. A heavily subsidized heavy water plant operated briefly in Glace Bay during the 1970s but soon closed down as well. DEVCO now operates two high tech coal mines, on the outskirts of New Waterford and Sydney Mines, producing less than a third of the earlier levels of output and employing only a tiny fraction of the former workforce. Its coal is burned in thermal power plants in the province or exported to other parts of the world; none of it now forms part of either a regional or a national industrial strategy.

The Sydney Steel Corporation (SYSCO) was incorporated as a provincial crown corporation in 1968 to take over the aging steel plant after Dominion Coal and Steel announced closure. In 1984, it employed about 1,300 workers, down from the more than 5,000 employed at its peak during the war. In 1991, after all of its basic steel making capacity had shut down for good, a mini-mill with an electric-

21. David Frank, "The Cape Breton Coal Industry…"; L.D. McCann, "The Mercantile-Industrial Transition in the Metals Towns of Pictou County, 1857–1931," in *Acadiensis* X, 2 (Spring, 1981); Anders Sandberg, "Dependent Development…'
22. David Frank, "Company Town/Labour Town…"

arc furnace for melting scrap metal for rolling into steel rails was installed at great expense, it employed just 750 workers. In 1992, the Nova Scotia Government announced SYSCO would be sold to the highest bidder and its future remains in doubt.[23]

Pictou County

Like Cape Breton, Pictou County had a complex of coal mining and industrial towns surrounding Pictou harbour, though a more sizable portion the county's population was involved with agriculture as well. Steel products were produced in New Glasgow and Trenton from the 1880s onward, when the Nova Scotia Steel and Coal Company took advantage of National Policy tariffs. During the rapid expansion under the National Policy, its products were exported to other parts of the country. Coal mining more or less disappeared in the 1950s and 1960s, and much of the metal working is disappearing as well. When markets contracted, towns that depended upon steel and coal contracted, a process eased somewhat by the mobility of workers, who seemed able to move back and forth between rural and urban areas depending on the availability of jobs. Addition of a Michelin Tire Plant and the massive Scott International Company pulp and paper mill have diversified its industrial economy somewhat in recent decades.[24]

Figure IV.10   Urban/rural population change in Pictou County, 1871–1991

(Thousands of persons)

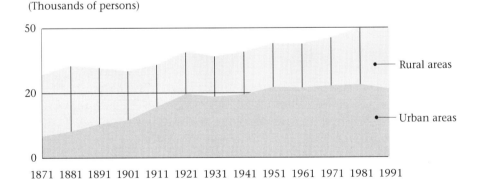

1871 1881 1891 1901 1911 1921 1931 1941 1951 1961 1971 1981 1991

Towns: New Glasgow, Pictou, Trenton, Stellarton, Westville.

23. Joan Bishop, "Sydney Steel: Public Ownership..."; Alan Tupper, "Public Enterprise as Social Welfare: The Case of the Cape Breton Development Corporation," in *Canadian Public Policy* 4, no. 4 (Autumn, 1978): 530–546.

24. James M. Cameron, *Industrial History of the New Glasgow District* (New Glasgow, 1963); L.D. McCann, "The Mercantile-Industrial Transition..."; Larry McCann and Jill Burnett, "Social Mobility and the Ironmasters of Late Nineteenth Century New Glasgow," in *People and Place: Studies of Small Town Life in the Maritimes*, L.D. McCann (ed.) (Fredericton, 1987); Larry McCann, "Living the Double Life..."; and Sandberg, "Dependent Development..."

Pictou achieved its maximum urban population in 1921, by which time the number of people in its towns had almost tripled from their small early position. By then they accommodated 60% of the county population. As with Cape Breton, the 1920s and 1930s brought stagnation. New Glasgow, Trenton, Stellarton and Westville owed everything to their coal and metals industries, which were largely associated with railway building. Pictou town, as county shire town, reaped the benefits of administering a county experiencing rapid growth. But no major manufacturing centres were located there.

Modern industries such as Michelin and Scott Paper exploit a set of urban infrastructures left behind after abandonment of the towns by former industries. They also take advantage of economic development incentives from various federal and provincial government agencies. Like many industries established in the region since the 1960s, these plants are located some distance from existing towns, taking advantage of lower land costs and major highway improvements to move both their supplies and work force in and out of their plants. One recent twist to development in the Pictou region is an accentuation of tourism that features a massive new museum of industry that will focus attention on the industrial history of the area, much like the Cape Breton Miner's Museum in Glace Bay does for that area.

Newfoundland Industrial Zones[25]

Newfoundland's mining industry began production on Bell Island when the Nova Scotia Coal and Steel Company began to mine iron ore for use in its Nova Scotia steel mills. A significant part of its production would be exported to the United States and Europe, but it was structurally tied directly to the larger developments occurring on Cape Breton. Between 1901 and 1915, output at the various Bell Island mines increased steadily. At Bell Island, workers and families lived in a company town structured much like Nova Scotia's coal towns. Company-owned houses were built close to the mines and a shack-town developed on the outskirts for the more transient labourers who flocked to the mining town on a seasonal basis. The market for iron ore soared in the pre-World War I period but contracted considerably afterward. Wabana would continue to produce ore until the 1950s and a town emerged with many of the characteristics of Cape Breton's coal towns. The same management system and the same mind-set were put in

25. The following discussion is directed towards districts five and six, Humber and Central Newfoundland, which were not created until the 1921 census. Included as well is the district of Labrador. Bell Island, one of the earliest industrial communities in the province, is in the Avalon census district, so is incorporated within the urban element of that district.

Figure IV.11   Urban/rural population change in Central-Humber, Newfoundland, 1921–91

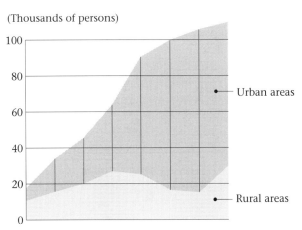

(Thousands of persons)

Towns: Corner Brook, Grand Falls/Windsor, Gander, Goose Bay, Labrador City/Wabush.

place to ensure that workers were available to take the iron ore out of the ground and get it shipped.[26]

Newfoundland developed a pulp and paper industry after 1900. Until then, the resources of the vast interior of the colony had been only little explored or exploited. Construction of the Newfoundland Railroad in the 1880s brought attention to forest and mineral reserves of the interior. Like the rest of Canada's boreal forest, Newfoundland's smaller conifers proved well adapted to pulp and paper-making. In the early 1900s, a pulp and paper industry emerged and wood products soon accounted for more than fourteen percent of Newfoundland's exports. Two major corporations obtained concessions from successive provincial governments in return for promises to develop industry and provide employment.

The most spectacular case of over-night urbanization around a pulp and paper mill in the entire region occurred at Corner Brook in western Newfoundland. In the 1920s, British investors and some of the Reid Newfoundland interests, the same group who had been responsible for constructing and operating the railway, built a huge pulp and paper mill there. In 1921, the Corner Brook area had a population of just over 1,000; by 1935, it approached 9,000. The social

26. Peter Neary, "'Traditional' and 'Modern' Elements in the Social and Economic History of Bell Island and Conception Bay," *CHA Historical Papers* (1973): 105–36; Gail Weir, *The Miners of Wabana: The Story of the Iron Ore Miners of Bell Island* (St. John's, 1989).

and economic impact on the area was massive. The Anglo-Newfoundland Development Company had earlier established a mill at Grand
Falls in 1909. It was one of the largest and most advanced in the world
and brought into existence a new urban conglomeration of Grand
Falls/Windsor/Bishop's Falls. Like Corner Brook, the Grand Falls plant
took advantage of a huge drainage basin and expanded very quickly.
Expansion of pulp making through the 1930s provided some of the
few opportunities for employment in Newfoundland.[27]

Because of these new population concentrations, two new census
districts were carved from existing coastal zones in the 1921 census.
From the very beginning, they approximated the urban-rural proportions of industrial zones in Nova Scotia and New Brunswick. Grand
Falls and Corner Brook evolved as company towns, though little
attention was paid to the housing of workers as in the coal towns of
Cape Breton and Pictou. The towns grew rather haphazardly on sites
adjacent to the mills where the bulk of the community worked (see
Fig. IV.11).

Development of the interior town of Gander during World War II
underscored the urban nature of the Central District. In the post-war
era, Gander continued to be largely a service centre for the huge airport located there. Labrador is included in the industrial zone because
its urban/rural profile came to mimic that of other industrial zones
after World War II. Prior to establishment of Goose Bay/Happy Valley
and Wabush/Labrador City after the war, Labrador's tiny permanent
population had been located along a long and sinuous coast-line. Like
the airport town of Gander, Happy Valley/Goose Bay owed its existence to the exigencies of war and the new power of airplanes.
Wabush/Labrador City is focused on mining iron ore and transporting
it out of the region by way of Quebec, to markets throughout North
America. Both communities were situated to serve a particular purpose
and carefully planned in the manner of post-war towns across the
country.

Industrial expansion and investment between 1880 and 1920 had
resulted in rapid population increases for a number of towns in the
region. The experience of industrial transformation was uneven across
the spectrum of towns, but the implications were similar in most circumstances. The arrival of large scale pulp and paper making somewhat later than the coal and steel based industrial expansion of the
earlier period created a new sort of town in the wilderness. Rapid

27.   Hiller, "The Origins of the Pulp & Paper Industry in Newfoundland."

Figure IV.12   Population change in selected towns, 1951–91

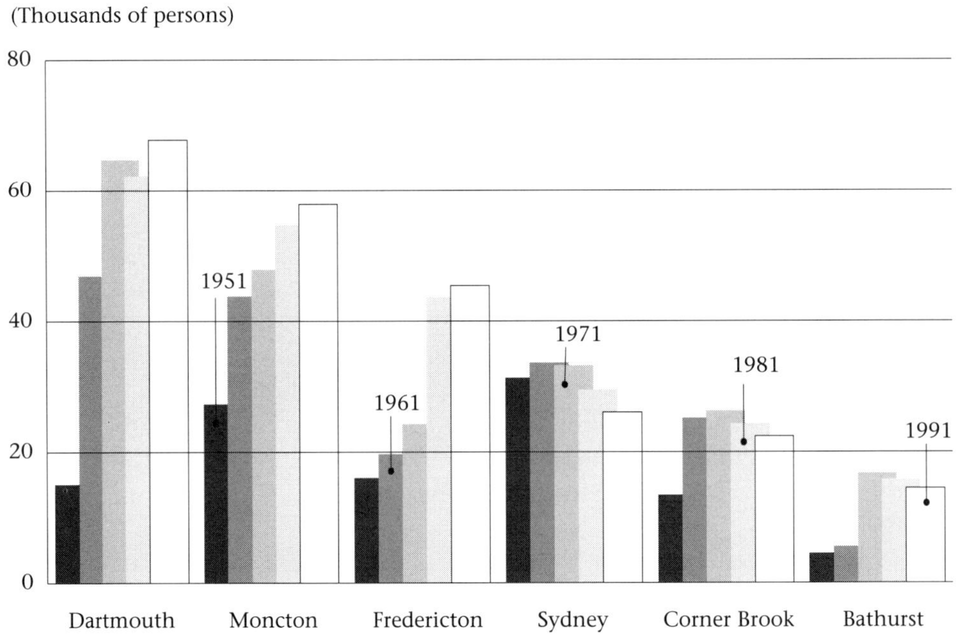

(Thousands of persons)

growth and subsequent stagnation have been characteristic of both experiences.

Industrial decline and out-migration after 1920 are reflected both in overall declines in population and fluctuating urban/rural ratios. State intervention has slowed this decline, but has not reversed it. Yet, well over 60% of the population of the four major industrial zones discussed here continue to live in urban centres, the locus for some of the more persistent social problems of the region.

Chapter V

Conclusion

A recurring theme in analyses of Atlantic Canada's development has been the absence of a dominant regional metropolis. Relations between this deficiency and the region's relatively slower economic growth and lack of persistent industrial development is at the centre of an ongoing debate. Much scholarship explaining Atlantic Canada's divergence from paths followed by central Canada revolves round the failure to successfully adapt to opportunities offered by modern capitalism. Explanations range from emphasis on the tyranny of location or limited resource endowment to the failure of local mercantile elites to adapt to the complexities of industrial capitalism.

While the patterns revealed by our data show a wide variety of urban configurations, the general trend across the region has been toward an integration of the more disparate system that had existed in the colonial phase. The relatively low position of regional cities and towns in any national hierarchy of urban prominence and power does not lessen their impact on the lives of people of the region and the fact that urbanization of the region as a whole continues to be as much as 20% below Canadian rates need not mean a failure to adapt to modernity.

Atlantic Canada's towns and cities derive their character as much from their particular local circumstances as from the larger political or economic milieu. They form a peculiar amalgam of the individual life experiences of their residents, who bring to their urban lives elements of various rural and foreign backgrounds. The broad trends towards modernization effecting the whole of western society has had an impact, but has been moderated by the resiliency of local cultures. Attempts by boosters to attract external capital or influence policies of both federal and provincial governments have had a dramatic impact on the course of each town's life, but reminders of local experiences that pervade each town's history are everywhere displayed in their history and present circumstances.

Once urbanized though, communities tend to remain so, even if their circumstances may vary and economic change may cause their populations to stagnate or even fall. In fact, urban development is profoundly influenced by extra-regional factors and intimately related to the region's political-economy. Since Confederation in 1867 central Canada has been the most important force for change in the region.

Towns and cities emerged at different stages of the region's history in response to different stimuli, creating a patchwork of communities. Our typology of four varieties of urbanization across the region represents one approach to analyzing such local contexts. In concentrating on the process of urbanization, rather than its end result, we uncovered a much different picture than could be obtained by simply measuring numbers, or simply comparing Atlantic Canada's experience to other models. Service and transportation networks had developed within the various zones independent of one another, resulting in a system without the clear hierarchical character so common to central and western Canada, where, from a much earlier date, transportation and staples export development was coordinated by government.

While it is partly true that Atlantic Canada is primarily a region of small towns, it is also a fact that service centres and resource-processing communities of the littoral and agricultural areas have been a vital and enduring part of its urban life. The persistence of resource enclaves that are directed from outside either the individual community or even the region in many cases has had a profound effect on its urban patterns. Profits from resource exploitation industries that form the economic base of such enclaves typically are controlled by outsiders. As a result, such industries, and the communities depended on them, experience a declining capacity for self-renewal. Another consequence, of course, has been the increased dependence on transfer payments to compensate for capitalism's failure to revitalize communities. Public involvement in the process of urbanization, ie. the transfer of a portion of the wealth produced to developing the urban infrastructures necessary for further growth, has characterized development of towns across the region.

Service towns in predominantly rural agricultural and coastal zones have remained relatively stable, continuing to serve their surrounding populations where occupational patterns and ways of life have undergone a considerable change. Fish-processing and pulp and paper towns have always depended on markets outside the region for disposal of their products. The control exercised by outside capitalists over development decisions within such communities has become more and more powerful. As the structure of those industries has become more concentrated in the hands of outsiders over the past fifty years, outside capitalists, whose interests in profit margins does not always coincide with the interests of their host communities, are powerfully situated to influence both government and local people regarding the direction of urban development.

Industrial towns along the Moncton-Sydney corridor have been equally vulnerable to the ups and downs of the manufacturing sector within the country, with its powerful trend towards consolidation at the centre. They expanded rapidly, investing heavily in both the modern technologies needed to compete in the manufacturing sectors and in the urban infrastructure needed to attract capital. During the period of national expansion, when railways were built and the National Policy was implemented, they led the way in the regional economy, drawing people and resources into their communities as never before. In the difficult times that followed World War I, as their manufacturing economies stagnated, the local elites of these communities were forced to lower their expectations of growth and prosperity.

Like the industrial towns, Halifax and Saint John have been directly affected by changing policies of the national government. However, the region's metropolitan centres, though more responsive to political and economic change than rural centres, have been able to retain, in fact to expand, their function and status vis à vis their hinterlands. Halifax's dominance of mainland Nova Scotia, for instance, has been reinforced by the growth of the provincial and federal bureaucracies there, the construction of a formidable network of highways of which it is the hub, as well as by the requirements of its own very large population. And St. John's remains the administrative and commercial centre of Newfoundland, and in recent years has come to house a huge portion of the provincial population in its complex of suburbs. Saint John's comparable position in New Brunswick is weakened, as it has long been, by the existence of Moncton and Fredericton, rival centres which perform distributive, government and administrative functions much like its own. However, as New Brunswick's major port and its industrial centre, Saint John maintains a precarious leadership over the province. Moncton and Fredericton meanwhile have profited, as has Charlottetown, from the post-War expansion of government activities.

Each of the metropolitan areas has attempted to modernize and renew its core area since the 1960s. In Halifax, this produced the destruction of a number of older neighbourhoods, the most notorious case being that of Africville, which combined an undeniable element of racism with disregard for existing working-class neighbourhoods. At the same time, the push for redevelopment produced the Historic Properties development along the decaying waterfront area, which has become the model for rejuvenation of the city. Similarly, Saint John's Market Square anchors new development in its downtown area.

As in other parts of North America, the decline of established central business districts has been a cause for concern. Renovation of downtown areas has been one response to the growth of suburban shopping malls as centres of retail activity in areas easily accessible by highways to rural, suburban, and city dwellers alike. By refurbishing their central business districts, cities seek both to counter this competition and appeal to tourists. In Moncton, period-style lamp-posts have been erected and a number of streets re-surfaced with cobblestones in an effort to stress the city's historic nature.

Charlottetown now emphasizes its 19th century architecture as a dramatic selling point for its tourist environment. But the malls on its outskirts, like shopping malls everywhere, have national chain stores anchoring their development. Strip malls, with their rows of fast food franchises and chain motels, greet visitors on their way into town, just as they do everywhere else. These malls and the strip developments that accompany them compete with historical ones as attractions for the people of both the towns and cities themselves and of the surrounding countrysides.

The reclamations of older parts of urban central business districts for retail and commercial purposes reflects the recent importance of tourism to the regional economy. Tourist strategies now combine the region's natural beauty and historic and cultural ambience with an image of its safe and clean urban spaces. Local merchants and the governments of most cities and towns strive to develop tourist attractions in whatever way they can. Even the recent industrial past is marketed as an attraction, as derelict industrial sites are refurbished as tourist attractions in old coal-mining towns like Springhill and Glace Bay and in Stellarton's new Museum of Industry, a joint project of the federal and provincial governments.

From another perspective, growth of the malls continues a trend discernible since earlier in this century: extension of central Canadian branch businesses into the region. Economies of scale give national chains located in new malls an additional advantage over local retailers, thereby enabling them to challenge the limited hegemony of regionally based retailers.

A related trend promoted as a development strategy has seen the construction of large, multi-purpose arenas with vast amounts of public money. In order to maintain the carrying charges of such complexes, cities need activities. Hence, new the presence in the region of teams in professional hockey and basketball leagues. These teams are staffed by athletes under contract to organizations based in "major league" cities outside the region, emphasizing once again the satellite status of regional centres. As well the new centres offer many possibilities for hosting tours of travelling versions of spectacles from the heartlands of North America .

In spite of the pervasiveness of cosmopolitan cultural norms, identification of residents with their towns of origin continues to be strong. This is partly due to a political history which has produced four distinct sets of judicial, political, and municipal institutions and partly a consequence of the specific experience of each town. The urban culture of the region remains highly varied, in keeping with the diverse, some would say "fragmented", character of its geography and population.

The affinity of residents to their towns is more than purely economic. Ethnicity and religion undoubtedly influence town and city self awareness as well, though the dimensions of this phenomenon remain largely unexplored. While the attention of "boosters", officials, and politicians has focused on problems of economic growth and how best to attract capital to their areas, the region's towns-people have more often concentrated on the problems and pleasures of everyday life. Recent refurbishment of downtowns, intended to attract tourists, provides centres for restaurants and other amenities enjoyed by all who live within these communities.

Multipurpose arenas that were designed to enhance competition between cities also provide entertainment centres and gathering places for inhabitants of surrounding rural areas, as well as for residents of the cities themselves. And not just the larger cities have profited from the building boom in arenas and other facilities. Today a network of community arenas and entertainment facilities allow for more community interaction across the region at a wider variety of levels than ever before.

While economic power today is often centred elsewhere, the region's urban places continue to maintain their importance in the lives of the region's people, even if those functions seem directed towards serving as intermediaries for larger urban and social systems within the Canadian fabric. The larger urban centres that, in growing and responding to the economic and political challenges presented by the region's history, have been more central to the development of its economy, ethos, and sense of identity. The functions that these metropolises perform for the region, helping to organize its economies, focus its views, and deal with outside forces on its behalf, are frequently performed by residents of larger centres.

Appendix

Population of Various Urban Centres in the Atlantic Provinces, 1871–1991

Urban centre	County	1871	1881	1891	1901	1911	1921	1931	1941
New Brunswick									
Atholville	Restigouche	–	–	–	–	–	–	–	–
Balmoral	Restigouche	–	–	–	–	–	–	–	–
Bas-Caraquet	Gloucester	–	–	–	–	–	–	–	–
Bathurst	Gloucester	–	–	–	1,044	960	3,327	3,300	3,554
Beresford	Gloucester	–	–	–	–	–	–	–	–
Bertrand	Gloucester	–	–	–	–	–	–	–	–
Blacks Harbour	Charlotte	–	–	–	–	–	–	–	–
Bouctouche	Kent	–	–	–	–	–	–	–	–
Campbellton	Restigouche	–	–	1,782	2,652	3,817	5,570	6,505	6,748
Cap-Pele	Westmorland	–	–	–	–	–	–	–	–
Caraquet	Gloucester	–	–	–	–	–	–	–	–
Charlo	Restigouche	–	–	–	–	–	–	–	–
Chatham	Northumberland	–	–	4,868	4,666	4,506	4,017	4,082	
Chipman	Queens	–	–	–	–	–	–	–	
Dalhousie	Restigouche	–	–	–	862	1,650	1,958	3,974	4,508
Devon	York	–	–	–	–	–	1,921	1,977	2,337
Dieppe	Westmorland	–	–	–	–	–	–	–	–
Doaktown	Northumberland	–	–	–	–	–	–	–	–
Dorchester	Westmorland	–	–	–	–	–	–	–	–
Douglastown	Northumberland	–	–	–	–	–	–	–	–
East Riverside-Kingshurst,	Kings	–		–	–		–	–	–
Edmundston	Madawaska	–	–	–	–	1,821	4,035	6,430	7,096
Eel River Crossing	Restigouche	–		–	–	–	–	–	–
Fairvale.	Kings	–	–	–	–	–	–	–	–
Fredericton	York	6,006	6,218	6,502	7,117	7,208	8,114	8,830	10,062
Gondola Point	Kings	–	–	–	–	–	–	–	–
Grand Bay	Kings	–	–	–	–	–	–	–	–
Grand Falls	Victoria	–	–	530	644	1,280	1,327	1,556	1,806
Hampton	Kings	–	–	–	–	–	–	–	–
Hartland	Carleton	–	–	–	–	–	879	907	847
Hillsborough	Albert	–	–	–	–	–	–	–	–
Kedgewick	Restigouche	–	–	–	–	–	–	–	–
Lameque	Gloucester	–	–	–	–	–	–	–	–
Lancaster	Saint John	–	–	–	–	–	–	–	–
Marysville	York	–	–	1,339	1,892	1,837	1,614	1,512	1,651
McAdam	York	–	–	–	–	–	–	–	–
Milltown	Charlotte	–	1,664	2,146	2,044	1,804	1,976	1,735	1,876
Minto	Queens	–	–	–	–	–	–	–	–
Moncton, Westmorland		600	5,032	8,765	9,026	11,345	17,488	20,689	22,763
Nackawic	York	–	–	–	–	–	–	–	–

Urban centre	1951	1956	1961	1966	1971	1976	1981	1986	1991
New Brunswick									
Atholville	–	–	–	–	2,108	1,862	1,694	1,501	1,474
Balmoral	–	–	–	–	–	1,722	1,823	1,969	1,949
Bas-Caraquet	–	–	–	–	1,685	1,728	1,859	1,913	1,849
Bathurst	4,453	5,267	5,494	15,256	16,674	16,301	15,705	14,683	14,409
Beresford	–	–	–	–	2,325	3,199	3,652	3,851	4,367
Bertrand	–	–	–	–	1,094	1,203	1,268	1,279	1,310
Blacks Harbour	–	–	–	–	–	1,619	1,356	1,224	1,139
Bouctouche	–	–	–	–	1,964	2,556	2,476	2,420	2,364
Campbellton	7,754	8,389	9,873	10,175	10,335	9,282	9,818	9,073	8,699
Cap-Pele	–	–	–	–	2,081	2,287	2,199	2,261	2,181
Caraquet	–	–	–	3,047	3,441	3,950	4,315	4,493	4,556
Charlo	–	–	–	–	1,621	1,302	1,603	1,602	1,597
Chatham	5,223	6,332	7,109	8,136	7,833	7,601	6,779	6,219	6,544
Chipman	–	–	–	–	1,977	1,999	1,829	1,760	1,615
Dalhousie	4,939	5,468	5,856	6,107	6,255	5,640	4,958	5,363	4,775
Devon	–	–	–	–	–	–	–	–	–
Dieppe	3,402	3,876	4,032	3,847	4,277	7,460	8,511	9,084	10,463
Doaktown	–	–	–	–	938	1,022	1,009	999	1,090
Dorchester	–	–	–	–	1,199	1,125	1,101	1,198	848
Douglastown	–	–	–	–	637	1,032	1,091	1,133	1,556
East Riverside-Kingshurst	–	–	–	–	852	1,042	989	1,031	1,049
Edmundston	10,753	11,997	12,791	12,517	12,365	12,710	12,044	11,497	10,835
Eel River Crossing	–	–	–	–	1,075	811	1,431	1,479	1,467
Fairvale	–	–	–	–	2,050	3,258	3,960	4,660	5,041
Fredericton	16,018	18,303	19,683	22,460	24,254	45,248	43,723	44,352	46,466
Gondola Point	–	–	–	–	850	1,846	3,076	3,596	4,218
Grand Bay	–	–	–	–	–	2,947	3,173	3,319	3,613
Grand Falls	2,365	3,672	3,983	4,158	4,516	6,223	6,203	6,209	6,083
Hampton	–	–	–	–	1,748	2,641	3,141	3,405	3,590
Hartland	1,000	1,022	1,025	1,034	1,009	974	846	917	890
Hillsborough	–	–	–	–	781	1,153	1,239	1,214	1,239
Kedgewick	–	–	–	–	1,065	1,271	1,222	1,129	1,118
Lameque	–	–	–	–	933	973	1,571	1,806	1,687
Lancaster	–	12,371	13,848	15,836	–	–	–	–	–
Marysville	2,152	2,538	3,233	3,572	3,872	–	–	–	–
McAdam	–	–	–	–	2,224	1,985	1,857	1,658	1,600
Milltown	2,267	1,975	1,892	1,952	1,893	–	–	–	–
Minto	–	–	–	–	3,880	3,714	3,399	3,197	3,096
Moncton	27,334	36,003	43,840	45,847	47,891	55,934	54,743	55,468	57,010
Nackawic	–	–	–	–	1,324	1,341	1,357	1,288	1,224

Urban centre	County	1871	1881	1891	1901	1911	1921	1931	1941
Nashwaaksis	York	–	–	–	–	–	–	–	–
Neguac	Northumberland	–	–	–	–	–	–	–	–
Nelson-Miramichi	Northumberland	–	–	–	–	–	–	–	–
Newcastle	Northumberland	–	–	2,507	2,945	3,507	3,383	3,781
Nigadoo	Gloucester	–	–	–	–	–	–	–	–
Norton	Kings	–	–	–	–	–	–	–	–
Oromocto	Sunbury	–	–	–	–	–	–	–	–
Perth-Andover	Victoria	–	–	–	–	–	–	–	–
Petit Rocher	Gloucester	–	–	–	–	–	–	–	–
Le Goulet	Gloucester	–	–	–	–	–	–	–	–
Petitcodiac	Westmorland	–	–	–	–	–	–	–	–
Plaster Rock	Victoria	–	–	–	–	–	–	–	–
Pointe-Verte	Gloucester	–	–	–	–	–	–	–	–
Quispamsis	Kings	–	–	–	–	–	–	–	–
Renforth	Kings	–	–	–	–	–	–	–	–
Richibucto	Kent	–	–	–	–	–	–	–	–
Riverview	Albert	–	–	–	–	–	–	–	–
Riviere Verte	Madawaska	–	–	–	–	–	–	–	–
Rogersville	Northumberland	–	–	–	–	–	–	–	–
Rothesay	Kings	–	–	–	–	–	–	515	529
Sackville	Westmorland	–	–	–	1,444	2,039	2,173	2,234	2,489
Saint John, Saint John		41,325	41,353	39,179	40,711	42,511	47,166	47,514	51,741
Saint-Antoine	Kent	–	–	–	–	–	–	–
Saint-Basile	Madawaska	–	–	–	–	–	–	–	–
Saint-Jacques	Madawaska	–	–	–	–	–	–	–
Saint-Leonard	Madawaska						862	945	1,095
Saint-Louis de Kent	Kent	–	–	–	–	–	–	–	–
Saint-Quentin	Restigouche	–	–	–	–	–	–	–	–
Sainte-Anne de Madawaska, Madawaska					–	–	–	–	–
Salisbury	Westmorland	–	–	–	–	–	–	–	–
Shediac	Westmorland	–	–	–	1,075	1,442	1,973	1,883	2,147
Sheila	Gloucester	–	–	–	–	–	–	–	–
Shippegan	Gloucester	–	–	–	–	–	–	–	–
St. Andrews	Charlotte	–	–	–	1,064	987	1,065	1,207	1,167
St. George	Charlotte	–	–	–	733	988	1,110	1,087	1,169
St. Stephen	Charlotte	–	2,338	2,680	2,840	2,836	3,452	3,437	3,306
Ste-Marie/Ste Raphael	Gloucester	–	–	–	–	–	–	–	–
Sunny Brae	Westmorland	–	–	–	–	–	1,171	1,364	1,368
Sussex Corner	Kings	–	–	–	–	–	–	–	–
Sussex	Kings	–	–	–	1,398	1,906	2,198	2,252	3,027
Tide Head	Restigouche	–	–	–	–	–	–	–	–
Tracadie	Gloucester	–	–	–	–	–	–	–	–
Westfield	Kings	–	–	–	–	–	–	–	–
Woodstock	Carleton	2,282	2,487	3,288	3,644	3,856	3,380	3,259	3,593

Prince Edward Island

Alberton	Prince	–	–	–	–	–	625	590	554
Bunbury	Queens	–	–	–	–	–	–	–	–
Charlottetown	Queens	7,872	10,345	10,098	10,718	9,883	10,814	12,361	14,821

Urban centre	1951	1956	1961	1966	1971	1976	1981	1986	1991
Nashwaaksis	–	–	–	–	7,353	–	–	–	–
Neguac	–	–	–	–	1,498	1,733	1,755	1,754	1,745
Nelson-Miramichi	–	–	–	–	1,580	1,543	1,452	1,407	1,387
Newcastle	4,248	4,670	5,236	5,911	6,460	6,423	6,284	5,804	5,711
Nigadoo	–	–	–	–	597	799	1,075	974	950
Norton	–	–	–	–	1,149	1,285	1,372	1,442	1,476
Oromocto	–	661	12,170	14,112	11,427	10,276	9,064	9,656	9,325
Perth-Andover	–	–	–	–	2,108	1,973	1,872	1,889	1,877
Petit Rocher	–	–	–	–	1,624	1,790	1,860	1,924	1,988
Le Goulet	–	–	–	–	–	–	–	–	1,087
Petitcodiac	–	–	–	–	1,569	1,472	1,401	1,355	1,342
Plaster Rock	–	–	–	–	1,331	1,368	1,222	1,232	1,246
Pointe-Verte	–	–	–	–	524	617	1,335	1,257	1,193
Quispamsis	–	–	–	–	2,215	4,968	6,022	7,185	8,446
Renforth	–	–	–	–	1,606	1,572	1,490	1,452	1,474
Richibucto	–	–	–	–	1,850	1,909	1,722	1,609	1,469
Riverview	–	–	–	–	–	14,177	14,907	15,638	16,270
Riviere Verte	–	–	–	–	1,657	1,009	1,054	978	988
Rogersville	–	–	–	–	1,077	1,138	1,237	1,273	1,385
Rothesay	896	802	782	893	1,038	1,283	1,764	1,605	1,647
Sackville	2,873	2,849	3,038	3,186	3,180	5,755	5,654	5,470	5,494
Saint John	50,779	52,491	55,153	51,567	89,039	85,956	80,521	76,381	74,969
Saint-Antoine	–	–	–	–	756	1,062	1,217	1,328	1,380
Saint-Basile	–	–	–	–	3,085	3,072	3,214	3,306	3,332
Saint-Jacques	–	–	–	–	1,072	1,374	2,297	2,310	2,505
Saint-Leonard	1,419	1,593	1,666	1,635	1,478	1,593	1,566	1,512	1,545
Saint-Louis de Kent	–	–	–	–	992	1,278	1,166	1,101	1,009
Saint-Quentin	–	–	–	–	2,093	2,246	2,334	2,264	2,269
Sainte-Anne de Madawaska	–	–	–	–	1,253	1,341	1,332	1,294	1,341
Salisbury	–	–	–	–	1,070	1,410	1,672	1,742	1,805
Shediac	2,010	2,173	2,159	2,134	2,203	4,216	4,285	4,370	4,343
Sheila	–	–	–	–	–	–	1,172	1,265	1,368
Shippegan	1,181	1,362	1,631	1,741	2,043	2,344	2,471	2,801	2,760
St. Andrews	1,458	1,534	1,531	1,719	1,812	1,711	1,760	1,612	1,652
St. George	1,263	1,322	1,133	1,104	977	1,148	1,163	1,305	1,345
St. Stephen	3,769	3,491	3,380	3,285	3,409	5,264	5,120	5,032	4,931
Ste-Marie/Ste Raphael	–	–	–	–	–	–	–	–	1,201
Sunny Brae	2,048	–	–	–	–	–	–	–	–
Sussex Corner	–	–	–	–	700	864	1,023	1,295	1,346
Sussex	3,224	3,403	3,457	3,607	3,942	3,938	3,972	4,114	4,132
Tide Head	–	–	–	–	797	897	952	1,085	1,156
Tracadie	–	–	–	2,018	2,222	2,591	2,452	2,444	2,619
Westfield	–	–	–	–	461	1,048	1,100	1,113	1,203
Woodstock	3,996	4,308	4,305	4,442	4,846	4,869	4,649	4,549	4,631

Prince Edward Island

	1951	1956	1961	1966	1971	1976	1981	1986	1991
Alberton	674	820	855	796	973	1,062	1,020	1,103	1,068
Bunbury	–	–	–	–	527	759	1,024	1,054	1,251
Charlottetown	15,887	16,707	18,318	18,427	19,133	17,063	15,282	15,776	15,396

Urban centre	County	1871	1881	1891	1901	1911	1921	1931	1941
Cornwall	Queens	–	–	–	–	–	–	–	–
East Royalty	Queens	–	–	–	–	–	–	–	–
Georgetown	Kings	–	–	–	–	–	719	679	769
Hillsborough Park	Queens	–	–	–	–	–	–	–	–
Kensington	Prince	–	–	–	–	–	556	612	767
Montague	Kings	–	–	–	–	–	706	803	769
Parkdale	Queens	–	–	–	–	–	–	–	–
St. Eleanors	Prince	–	–	–	–	–	–	–	–
Sherwood	Queens	–	–	–	–	–	–	–	–
Souris	Kings	–	–	–	1,140	1,089	1,094	1,063	1,114
Southport	Queens	–	–	–	–	–	–	–	–
Summerside	Prince	1,917	2,853	2,882	2,875	2,678	3,228	3,759	5,034
Tignish	Prince	–	–	–	–	–	–	–	–
West Royalty	Queens	–	–	–	–	–	–	–	–
Wilmot	Prince	–	–	–	–	–	–	–	–
Winsloe	Queens	–	–	–	–	–	–	–	–

Nova Scotia

Urban centre	County	1871	1881	1891	1901	1911	1921	1931	1941
Amherst, Cumberland		1,839	2,274	3,781	4,964	8,973	9,998	7,450	8,620
Annapolis Royal	Annapolis	–	–	–	1,019	1,019	836	739	782
Antigonish	Antigonish	–	–	693	1,838	1,787	1,746	1,764	2,157
Bedford	Halifax	–	–	–	–	–	–	–	–
Berwick	Kings	–	–	–	–	–	–	837	962
Bridgetown, Annapolis		974	1,058	1,117	858	996	1,086	1,126	1,020
Bridgewater, Lunenburg		1,687	2,026	2,234	2,203	2,340	3,147	3,262	3,445
Canso, Guysborough		704	900	1,131	1,479	1,617	1,626	1,575	1,418
Clark's Harbour	Shelburne	–	–	–	665	883	965	907	887
Dartmouth	Halifax	2,191	3,786	4,452	4,806	5,058	7,899	9,100	10,847
Digby	Digby	942	1,278	1,381	1,150	1,247	1,230	1,412	1,657
Dominion	Cape Breton	–	–	–	1,546	2,589	2,390	2,846	3,279
Glace Bay	Cape Breton	–	–	2,459	6,945	16,562	17,007	20,706	25,147
Halifax, Halifax		29,582	36,100	38,437	40,832	46,619	58,372	59,275	70,488
Hantsport	Hants	–	–	–	–	–	683	704	907
Inverness	Inverness	–	–	–	306	2,719	2,963	2,900	2,975
Joggins	Cumberland	–	–	–	1,088	1,648	1,732	1,000	1,109
Kentville, Kings		1,779	2,125	1,686	1,731	2,304	2,717	3,033	3,928
Liverpool, Queens		2,204	2,224	2,046	1,937	2,109	2,294	2,669	3,170
Lockeport, Shelburne		1,011	1,228	1,220	1,117	784	851	973	1,084
Louisbourg, Cape Breton		1,446	999	1,116	1,046	1,006	1,152	971	1,012
Lunenburg, Lunenburg		1,777	2,204	2,692	2,916	2,681	2,792	2,727	2,856
Mahone Bay	Lunenburg	–	–	–	866	951	1,177	1,065	1,025
Middleton	Annapolis	–	–	–	537	827	875	904	1,172
Mulgrave	Guysborough	–	–	–	–	–	–	975	1,057
New Glasgow, Pictou		1,676	2,595	3,776	4,447	6,383	8,974	8,858	9,210
New Waterford	Cape Breton	–	–	–	–	–	5,615	7,745	9,302
North Sydney, Cape Breton		1,200	1,520	2,513	4,646	5,418	6,585	6,139	6,836
Oxford, Cumberland		1,034	1,249	1,427	1,285	1,392	1,402	1,133	1,297
Parrsboro	Cumberland	–	–	1,909	2,705	2,224	2,161	1,919	1,971
Pictou	Pictou	2,883	3,403	2,998	3,235	3,179	2,988	3,152	3,069

Urban centre	1951	1956	1961	1966	1971	1976	1981	1986	1991
Cornwall	–	–	–	–	657	1,256	1,838	1,894	2,038
East Royalty	–	–	–	–	–	–	1,696	2,039	2,052
Georgetown	762	754	744	826	767	732	737	729	716
Hillsborough Park	–	–	–	–	–	–	1,227	996	1,489
Kensington	811	854	884	1,022	1,086	1,150	1,143	1,105	1,332
Montague	1,068	1,152	1,126	1,289	1,608	1,827	1,957	1,994	1,901
Parkdale	–	1,422	1,735	2,071	2,313	2,172	2,018	2,065	2,198
St. Eleanors	–	–	1,002	1,419	1,621	2,495	2,716	3,743	3,514
Sherwood	–		1,580	2,436	3,807	5,602	5,681	5,769	6,006
Souris	1,183	1,449	1,537	1,443	1,393	1,447	1,413	1,379	1,333
Southport	–	–	–	–	–	1,009	1,313	1,321	1,665
Summerside	6,547	7,242	8,611	10,042	9,439	8,592	7,828	8,020	7,474
Tignish	–	914	994	982	1,060	1,077	982	960	893
West Royalty	–	–	–	–	–	–	1,686	2,070	3,142
Wilmot	–	–	–	619	737	1,183	1,563	1,708	2,176
Winsloe	–	–	–	–	–	–	1,067	1,123	1,105

Nova Scotia

Urban centre	1951	1956	1961	1966	1971	1976	1981	1986	1991
Amherst	9,870	10,301	10,788	10,551	9,966	10,263	9,684	9,671	9,742
Annapolis Royal	784	765	800	805	758	738	631	631	633
Antigonish	3,196	3,592	4,344	4,856	5,489	5,442	5,205	5,291	4,924
Bedford	–		–	–	4,759	4,977	6,777	8,010	11,618
Berwick	1,045	1,134	1,282	1,311	1,412	1,701	1,699	2,058	2,150
Bridgetown	1,038	1,041	1,043	1,060	1,039	1,037	1,047	1,118	1,021
Bridgewater	4,010	4,445	4,497	4,755	5,231	6,010	6,669	6,617	7,248
Canso	1,313	1,261	1,151	1,190	1,209	1,173	1,255	1,285	1,228
Clark's Harbour	1,020	945	945	1,002	1,082	1,077	1,059	1,098	1,076
Dartmouth	15,037	21,093	46,966	58,745	64,770	65,341	62,277	65,243	67,798
Digby	2,047	2,145	2,308	2,305	2,363	2,542	2,558	2,525	2,311
Dominion	3,143	2,964	2,999	2,960	2,879	2,938	2,856	2,754	2,517
Glace Bay	25,586	24,416	24,186	23,516	22,440	21,836	21,466	20,467	19,501
Halifax	85,589	93,301	92,511	86,792	122,035	117,882	114,594	113,577	114,455
Hantsport	1,131	1,298	1,381	1,438	1,447	1,423	1,395	1,357	1,274
Inverness	2,360	2,026	2,109	2,022	–	–	–	–	–
Joggins	–	–	–	–	–	–	–	–	–
Kentville	4,240	4,937	4,612	5,176	5,198	5,056	4,974	5,208	5,506
Liverpool	3,535	3,500	3,712	3,607	3,654	3,336	3,304	3,295	3,113
Lockeport	1,225	1,207	1,231	1,284	1,208	1,030	929	917	798
Louisbourg	1,120	1,314	1,417	1,617	1,582	1,519	1,410	1,355	1,261
Lunenburg	2,816	2,859	3,056	3,154	3,215	3,024	3,014	2,972	2,781
Mahone Bay	1,019	1,109	1,103	1,296	1,333	1,236	1,228	1,093	1,096
Middleton	1,506	1,769	1,921	1,765	1,870	1,823	1,834	1,772	1,819
Mulgrave	1,212	1,227	1,145	1,124	1,196	1,206	1,099	1,051	935
New Glasgow	9,933	9,998	9,782	10,489	10,849	10,672	10,464	10,022	9,905
New Waterford	10,423	10,381	10,592	9,725	9,579	9,223	8,808	8,326	7,695
North Sydney	7,354	8,125	8,657	8,752	8,604	8,319	7,820	7,472	7,260
Oxford	1,466	1,545	1,471	1,426	1,473	1,498	1,470	1,376	1,384
Parrsboro	1,906	1,849	1,834	1,835	1,807	1,857	1,799	1,729	1,634
Pictou	4,259	4,564	4,534	4,254	4,250	4,588	4,628	4,413	4,134

Urban centre	County	1871	1881	1891	1901	1911	1921	1931	1941
Port Hawkesbury	Inverness	–	–	658	633	684	869	1,011	1,031
Shelburne, Shelburne		1,423	1,155	1,300	1,445	1,435	1,360	1,474	1,605
Springhill	Cumberland	–	900	4,813	4,559	5,713	5,681	6,355	7,170
Stellarton	Pictou	1,750	1,599	2,410	2,335	3,910	5,312	5,002	5,351
Stewiacke	Colchester	–	–	–	–	–	819	803	961
Sydney, Cape Breton		1,700	2,180	2,427	9,909	17,723	22,545	23,089	28,305
Sydney Mines, Cape Breton		1,494	2,340	2,442	3,191	7,470	8,327	7,769	8,198
Trenton, Pictou		397	424	641	998	1,414	2,844	2,613	2,699
Truro, Colchester		2,114	3,461	5,102	5,993	6,107	7,562	7,901	10,272
Wedgeport	Yarmouth	–	–	–	1,026	1,392	1,424	1,294	1,327
Westville	Pictou	1,675	2,202	3,152	3,471	4,417	4,550	3,946	4,115
Windsor	Hants	2,281	2,536	2,830	2,849	2,894	2,946	3,032	3,436
Wolfville	Kings	1,697	1,880	1,963	1,412	1,458	1,743	1,818	1,944
Yarmouth, Yarmouth		2,500	3,485	6,089	6,430	6,600	7,073	7,055	7,790

Newfoundland

Arnold's Cove	Avalon Penin.	–	–	–	–	–	–	–	–
Badger's Quay[1]	Bonavista-Trinity	–	–	–	–	–	–	–	–
Badger	Central Nfld.	–	–	–	–	–	–	–	911
Baie Verte	Notre Dame Bay	–	–	–	–	–	–	–	282
Bay Bulls	Avalon Penin.	–	–	–	–	–	–	–	–
Bay Roberts, Avalon Penin.		2,367	2,763	2,177	2,226	2,187	2,168	1,911	1,301
Bishops' Falls	Central Nfld.	–	–	–	–	343	843	1,882	2,522
Bonavista Bonavista-Trinity		2,992	3,463	3,551	3,696	3,911	4,052	4,022	1,401
Botwood	Central Nfld.	–	–	–	541	852	1,018	1,090	2,744
Brigus, Avalon Penin.		1,975	2,365	1,541	1,162	1,034	935	886	888
Buchans	Central Nfld.	–	–	–	–	–	–	1,104	1,395
Burgeo	South Coast	–	–	723	807	1,039	993	823	750
Burin	Burin Penin.	–	–	2,729	2,719	2,783	2,763	2,277	709
Burnt Islands	South Coast	–	–	–	–	–	–	–	491
Carbonear, Avalon Penin.		4,358	3,756	4,127	3,703	3,540	3,320	3,367	3,472
Catalina	Bonavista-Trinity	–	1,647	1,470	1,016	651	609	629	
Channel (Port aux Basques), South Coast			–	–	1,052	1,223	1,502	2,010	2,178
Clarenville, Bonavista-Trinity		–	–	–	229	303	354	523	964
Clarke's Beach, Avalon Penin.		486	391	536	569	576	563	526	515
Conception Bay South, Avalon Penin.		–	–	–	–	–	–	–	–
Conception Hr., Avalon Penin.		704	855	878	932	988	892	812	685
Corner Brook	Humber	–	–	–	853	1,658	1,349	8,603	11,889
Deer Lake	Humber	–	–	–	–	–	–	1,227	1,927
Dunville	Avalon Penin.	–	–	–	–	–	–	–	287
Durrell	Notre Dame Bay	–	–	–	–	–	–	–	511
Englee	Northern Penin.	–	–	242	279	415	522	551	
Flatrock	Avalon Penin.	–	–	–	–	–	–	–	–
Fogo	Notre Dame Bay	–	1,020	1,118	1,152	1,216	1,164	1,044	
Fortune	Burin Penin.	–	786	809	937	917	934	960	909
Freshwater	Avalon Penin.	–	–	–	–	–	–	–	594
Gambo	Bonavista-Trinity	–	–	–	–	–	–	–	–
Gander	Central Nfld.	–	–	–	–	–	–	–	293
Glenwood	Central Nfld.	–	–	–	–	–	–	–	–

Urban centre	1951	1956	1961	1966	1971	1976	1981	1986	1991
Glovertown	–	604	1,197	1,246	1,915	2,176	2,165	2,184	2,276
Goulds	–	–	–	–	2,280	3,317	4,242	4,688	6,162
Grand Bank	2,148	2,430	2,703	3,143	3,476	3,802	3,901	3,732	3,528
Grand Falls[2]	5,064	6,064	6,605	7,451	7,677	8,729	8,765	9,121	14,693
Halfway Point and others	625	697	1,003	1,312	1,907	2,144	2,214	2,182	2,104
Happy Valley-Goose Bay	2,416	5,152	5,901	6,579	7,024	8,075	7,103	7,248	8,610
Harbour Breton	903	989	1,076	1,442	2,196	2,317	2,464	2,432	2,418
Harbour Grace	2,331	2,545	2,650	2,811	2,771	2,937	2,988	3,053	3,419
Harbour Main[3]	–	–	–	–	–	1,313	1,303	1,293	1,278
Hare Bay	719	1,195	1,467	1,410	1,485	1,598	1,520	1,436	1,387
Heart's Content	594	646	607	592	599	634	625	620	567
Holyrood	523	559	789	1,125	1,282	1,610	1,789	2,118	2,075
Irishtown-Summerside	–	–	–	–	–	–	–	–	1,560
Isle aux Morts	664	773	884	1,064	1,158	1,270	1,238	1,203	1,146
Jerseyside-Placentia Bay	544	713	923	953	1,061	1,027	641	764	715
Joe Batt's Arm[4]	1,252	1,455	1,483	1,345	1,176	1,023	1,155	1,232	1,164
Kippens	641	799	1,079	1,199	1,383	1,267	1,219	1,556	1,767
La Scie	601	702	939	1,064	1,255	1,256	1,422	1,429	1,412
Labrador City	–	–	386	5,037	7,622	12,012	11,538	8,664	9,061
Lawn	531	634	716	875	1,000	1,025	999	1,015	1,005
Lewisporte	1,218	2,076	2,702	2,892	3,175	3,782	3,963	3,978	3,848
Logy Bay[5]	–	–	–	–	–	–	–	–	1,882
Marystown	1,206	1,460	1,691	1,894	4,960	5,915	6,299	6,660	6,739
Milltown[6]	563	693	972	1,079	1,233	1,325	1,376	1,276	1,161
Mount Pearl	–	1,979	2,785	4,428	7,211	10,193	11,543	20,293	23,689
Musgrave Harbour	934	1,016	1,062	1,183	1,232	1,530	1,554	1,527	1,528
Nain	285	222	465	591	708	812	938	1,018	1,069
Norman'Cove-Long Cove	659	811	862	850	997	1,155	1,152	1,107	1,054
Norris Arm	1,126	976	1,226	1,252	1,191	1,342	1,216	1,127	1,089
North West River	511	563	753	835	931	1,022	515	526	528
Paradise	–	–	–	–	1,697	2,131	2,861	3,346	3,984
Pasadena	379	468	502	685	964	1,850	2,685	3,268	3,428
Peterview	558	618	726	836	953	1,099	1,119	1,130	1,011
Placentia	614	1,233	1,610	1,847	2,211	2,209	2,204	2,016	1,954
Port au Port West[7]	342	348	630	639	646	1,012	938	842	718
Port aux Choix	190	271	490	369	861	1,141	1,311	1,291	1,260
Portugal Cove	–	–	–	–	–	–	2,361	2,497	2,726
Pouch Cove	1,033	1,181	1,324	1,374	1,483	1,543	1,522	1,576	1,976
Ramea	714	931	970	1,160	1,208	1,226	1,386	1,380	1,224
Roberts Arm	406	606	750	993	1,044	1,064	1,005	1,111	994
Roddickton	892	1,062	1,185	1,227	1,239	1,234	1,142	1,223	1,153
Shoal Harbour	439	486	544	568	715	1,009	1,000	1,049	1,402
Spaniard's Bay	1,209	1,411	1,289	773	1,764	1,568	2,125	2,190	2,198
Springdale	1,543	2,130	2,795	2,773	3,224	3,513	3,501	3,555	3,545
St. Albans	1,079	1,334	1,547	1,715	1,941	2,040	1,968	1,780	1,586
St. Anthony	1,380	1,761	1,820	2,269	2,593	2,987	3,107	3,182	3,164
St. Georges	1,276	1,615	1,874	2,046	2,082	1,976	1,756	1,852	1,678
St. Jacques-Coomb's Cove	1,056	1,058	1,103	1,101	1,099	1,061	1,048	994	701
St. John's	52,873	57,078	63,633	79,884	88,102	86,576	83,770	96,216	95,770

Urban centre	County	1871	1881	1891	1901	1911	1921	1931	1941
St. Lawrence	Burin Penin.	–	–	–	799	842	803	832	1,251
St. Phillips	Avalon Penin.	–	–	–	–	–	–	–	–
Stephenville Crossing	St. Georges	–	–	–	112	156	267	512	956
Stephenville	St. Georges	–	–	–	643	826	817	926	871
Summerford	Notre Dame Bay		–	–	–	–	–	–	246
Torbay	Avalon Penin.	–	–	–	–	–	–	1,523	1,422
Trepassey	Avalon Penin.	–	–	–	–	–	–	–	–
Triton	Notre Dame Bay		–	–	–	–	–	–	–
Twillingate	Notre Dame Bay	3,071	3,694	3,585	3,542	3,348	3,217	3,203	933
Upper Island Cove	Avalon Penin.	–	–	–	799	802	901	942	1,080
Victoria	Avalon Penin.	–	–	–	818	999	1,101	1,044	1,099
Wabana	Avalon Penin.	–	–	–	–	–	–	–	–
Wabush	Labrador	–	–	–	–	–	–	–	–
Wedgewood Park	Avalon Penin.	–	–	–	–	–	–	–	–
Wesleyville	Bonavista-Trinity		–	–	456	781	1,105	1,182	968
Whitbourne	Avalon Penin.	–	–	–	643	400	412	520	607
Windsor	Central Nfld.	–	–	–	–	–	–	1,447	2,772
Winterton	Avalon Penin.		–	–	–	–	–	–	–
Witless Bay	Avalon Penin.		–	–	–	–	–	–	–

Urban centre	1951	1956	1961	1966	1971	1976	1981	1986	1991
St. Lawrence	1,451	1,837	2,095	2,130	2,173	2,258	2,012	1,841	1,743
St. Phillips	–	–	–	–	–	–	1,365	1,604	1,842
Stephenville Crossing	1,462	1,552	2,209	2,433	2,129	2,207	2,172	2,252	2,172
Stephenville	2,600	3,762	6,043	5,910	7,770	10,284	8,876	7,994	7,621
Summerford	682	788	878	889	996	1,099	1,198	1,169	1,157
Torbay	1,264	1,512	1,445	1,532	2,090	2,908	3,394	3,730	4,707
Trepassey	532	604	495	670	1,443	1,427	1,473	1,460	1,198
Triton	625	695	772	816	1,002	1,091	1,235	1,253	1,273
Twillingate	952	994	947	1,374	1,437	1,404	1,506	1,506	1,397
Upper Island Cove	1,346	1,563	1,668	1,790	1,819	1,851	2,025	2,055	2,038
Victoria	1,146	1,315	1,506	1,528	1,601	1,767	1,870	1,895	1,831
Wabana	6,460	7,873	8,026	7,884	5,421	4,824	4,254	4,057	3,608
Wabush	–	–	151	2,669	3,387	3,769	3,155	2,637	2,331
Wedgewood Park –	–	–	–	–	417	1,236	1,226	1,385	1,570
Wesleyville	1,304	1,313	1,285	1,238	1,142	1,167	1,225	1,208	1,126
Whitbourne	744	963	1,085	884	1,235	1,268	1,233	1,151	1,036
Windsor	3,674	4,520	5,505	6,692	6,644	6,349	5,747	5,545	–
Winterton	830	894	808	795	794	796	753	747	667
Witless Bay	–	–	–	–	–	–	–	1,022	1,064

Notes
1. Includes Valleyfield and Pool's Island.
2. 1991 figure includes Windsor.
3. Includes Chapel Cove and Lakeview.
4. Includes Barr'd Islands and Shoal Bay.
5. Includes Middle Cove and Outer Cove.
6. Includes Head of Baie d'Espoir.
7. Includes Aguathuna and Felix Cove.

Bibliography

Acheson, T.W. "The 'Great Merchant' and Economic Development in Saint John, 1820–1850." *Acadiensis* VIII, 2 (Spring 1979).

——. "The Maritimes and Empire Canada." *Canada and the Burden of Unity*, D.J. Bercuson (ed.). Toronto: Macmillan, 1977.

——. "The National Policy and the Industrialization of the Maritimes, 1880–1910." *Acadiensis* I, 2 (Spring 1972): 3–28.

——. *Saint John: The Making of a Colonial Urban Community*. Toronto: University of Toronto Press, 1985.

Adams, J. Gordon. *Urban Centres in New Brunswick*. Ottawa: Geographical Branch, 1968.

——. *Urban Centres in Newfoundland*. Ottawa: Department of Energy, Mines and Resources, 1967.

Aiton, Grace. *The Story of Sussex and Vicinity, 1967*. Sussex: Kings County Historical Society, 1979.

Albert, Thomas. *Histoire du Madawaska: Entre l'Acadie, le Québec et l'Amérique, 1920*. Québec: La Société Historique du Madawaska, Hurtubise HMH, 1982.

Alexander, David. "Development and Dependence in Newfoundland, 1880–1970." *Atlantic Canada and Confederation: Essays in Canadian Political Economy*. Toronto: University of Toronto Press, 1983.

——. "The Port of Yarmouth, Nova Scotia, 1840–1889." *Ships and Shipbuilding in the North Atlantic Region*, K. Matthews and G. Panting (eds.). St. John's: 1978.

Alexander, David and Gerry Panting. "The Mercantile Fleet and Its Owners: Yarmouth, Nova Scotia, 1840–1889." *Acadiensis* VII, 2 (Spring 1978): 3–28.

Alexander, David and Rosemary Ommer (eds.). *Volumes Not Values*. St. John's: Memorial University, Maritime History Group, 1980.

Anderson, Nels and R.E. Chateloup. "Leadership Roles of Cities." *The Problems of Leadership in Urban Communities*. University of New Brunswick, Division of Social Sciences. Saint John: Graphic Services, 1977.

Andrews, A. "Social Crisis and Labour Mobility: A Study of Economic and Social Change in a New Brunswick Railway Community." M.A. Thesis, University of New Brunswick, 1967.

Atlantic Provinces Economic Council. *The Atlantic Vision – 1990: A Development Strategy for the 1980s*. Halifax: Atlantic Provinces Economic Council, 1979.

——. *Some Economic and Social Characteristics of Charlotte County, New Brunswick*. Halifax: Atlantic Provinces Economic Council, March 1987.

Archibald, Bruce. "Atlantic Regional Underdevelopment and Socialism." *Essays on the Left,* L. Lapierre (ed.). Toronto: McClelland and Stewart, 1971.

Armstrong, C. and H.V.Nelles. "Getting Your Way in Nova Scotia: 'Tweaking' Halifax, 1909–1917." *Acadiensis* V, 2 (Spring 1976): 105–31.

Armstrong, Frederick H. *Bibliography of Canadian Urban History. Part II: The Atlantic Provinces*. Monticello, Illinois: Vance Bibliographies, 1980.

Artibise, Alan F.J. "Building Cities." *Building Canada: A History of Public Works*, Norman Ball (ed.). Toronto: University of Toronto Press, 1991.

——. "Patterns of Prairie Urban Development, 1871–1950." *Eastern and Western Perspectives*, P.A. Buckner and D.J. Bercuson (eds.). Toronto: University of Toronto Press, 1981.

Artibise, A.F.J. and M.J. Kiernan. *Canadian Regional Development: The Urban Dimension*. Local Development Paper No. 12. Ottawa: Economic Council of Canada, 1989.

Atlantic Development Board. *Urban Centres in the Atlantic Provinces*. Ottawa: Queen's Printer, 1967.

"Atlantic Provinces: Urban Growth for a Non-Urban Area." *Progressive Architecture* (September 1972): 108–11.

Axworthy, L. and James Gillies (eds.). *The City: Canada's Prospects, Canada's Problems*. Toronto: Butterworth, 1973.

Babcock, Robert. "The Saint John Street Railwaymen's Strike and Riot 1914." *Acadiensis* XI, 1 (Spring 1982): 3–27.

Bacher, John. "From Study to Reality: The Establishment of Public Housing in Halifax, 1930–1953." *Acadiensis* XVIII, 1 (Autumn 1988): 120–35.

Baillie, Murray. *Municipal Government in Metropolitan Halifax: A Bibliography*. Halifax: Saint Mary's University, 1977.

Bain, Douglas. "Simplified Urban Transportation Modelling: A Case Study of the Halifax-Dartmouth Area." M. Eng. Thesis, University of New Brunswick, 1983.

Baird, Frank (ed.). *The Story of Fredericton, 1848–1948: Fredericton's One Hundred Years*. Fredericton: Wilson, 1948.

Baird, William T. *Seventy Years of New Brunswick Life*. Fredericton: St. Annes Point Press, 1979.

Bairoch, Paul. *Cities and Economic Development: From the Dawn of History to the Present*. Chicago: University of Chicago Press, 1988.

Baker, John F. "The Underdevelopment of Atlantic Canada, 1867–1902: A Study of the Development of Capitalism." M.A. Thesis, McMaster University, 1977.

Baker, Melvin. "The Government of St. John's, Newfoundland, 1800–1921." Ph.D. Thesis, University of Western Ontario, 1981.

——. "Municipal Politics and Public Housing in St. John's, 1911–1921." *Workingmen's St. John's: Aspects of Social History in the Early 1900s*, Robert Cuff and William Earle Gillespie (eds.). St. John's: Cuff, 1982.

Baldwin, Douglas and Thomas Spira. *Gaslight, Epidemics and Vagabond Cows: Charlottetown in the Victorian Era*. Charlottetown: Ragweed Press, 1988.

Barrett, L.G. "Perspectives on Dependency and Underdevelopment in the Atlantic Region." *Canadian Review of Sociology and Anthropology* 17, 3 (August 1980): 273–86.

Bassler, Gerhard P. "'Develop or Perish': Joseph R. Smallwood and Newfoundland's Quest for German Industry, 1949–1953." *Acadiensis* XV, 2 (Spring 1986): 93–119.

Beaubien, Charles. *La population et la preservation des terres agricoles*. Ottawa: Conseil des sciences du Canada, 1978.

Bercuson, D.J. and P.A. Buckner (eds.). *Eastern and Western Perspectives*. Toronto: University of Toronto Press, 1981.

Bernard, A. et al. *Profile: Halifax-Dartmouth. The Political and Administrative structures of the Metropolitan Region of Halifax-Dartmouth*. Ottawa: Ministry of State for Urban Affairs, 1974.

Betcherman, Gordon. *Halifax-Dartmouth Journey-to-Work-Profile*. Ottawa: Economic Council of Canada, 1978.

Bettison, David George. *The Politics of Canadian Urban Development*. Edmonton: University of Alberta Press, 1975.

Bickerton, James. *Nova Scotia, Ottawa, and the Politics of Regional Development*. Toronto: University of Toronto Press, 1990.

——. "Regional Policy in Historical Perspective." *An Analysis of the Reorganization for Economic Development*. Halifax: Atlantic Provinces Economic Council, 1982.

——. "Regional Policy in Historical Perspective: The Federal Role in Regional Economic Development." *American Review of Canadian Studies* 14, 1 (1984).

——. "Underdevelopment and Social Movements in Atlantic Canada: A Critique." *Studies in Political Economy* 9 (Fall 1982): 191–202.

Bishop, Joan. "Sydney Steel: Public Ownership and the Welfare State, 1967–1975." *The Island: New Perspectives on Cape Breton's History, 1713–1990,* Kenneth Donovan (ed.). Fredericton: Acadiensis Press, 1990.

Blackmore, Laura. "Paper Town: Grand Falls." *Atlantic Guardian*. (1947).

Blom, Margaret Howard and Thomas Blom. *Canada Home: Juliana Horatia Ewing's Fredericton Letters*. Vancouver: University of British Columbia Press, 1983.

Bolger, Francis W.P. (ed.). *Canada's Smallest Province: A History of Prince Edward Island*. Charlottetown: P.E.I. Centennial Commission, 1973.

Boothroyd, P.D. "Urban Functional Organization in the Cape Breton Industrial Area." M.A. Thesis, University of Toronto, 1963.

Boswell, F. and C. Gillis. *The Story of the Department of Development, Province of Nova Scotia*. Halifax: Nova Scotia Department of Development, 1983.

Boucher, David N. "Metropolitan Growth in Atlantic Canada: Saint John and the Throughway." M.A. Thesis, Carleton University, 1993.

Bourne, L.S. *Canadian Settlement Trends: An Examination of the Spatial Pattern of Growth, 1971–1976*. Toronto: Centre for Urban and Community Studies, University of Toronto, 1979.

Boutelier, Ted (ed). *New Waterford, three score and ten: seventy years of civic history*. New Waterford, N.S.: Publication Committee, New Waterford 70th Anniversary, 1983.

Bradfield, Michael. "Michelin in Nova Scotia." *Working Canadians: Readings in the Sociology of Work and Industry*, G.S. Lowe and H.J. Krahn (eds.). Toronto: Methuen, 1984.

Brander, Peter. "The 'Political Economy of Management' and the Development of Dalhousie New Brunswick." M.A. Thesis, Carleton University, 1993

Bremner, Benjamin. "Memories of Long Ago: Being a Series of Sketches Pertaining to Charlottetown in the Past." Charlottetown: Irwin Printing, 1930.

Brenton, G.W. "Migration and Development in the Maritimes." M.A. Thesis, Queen's University, 1974.

Brookes, Alan. "Out-Migration from the Maritime Provinces, 1860–1900: Some Preliminary Considerations." *Acadiensis* V, 2 (Spring 1976): 26–55

Brown, James B. *Miracle Town: Springhill, Nova Scotia, 1790–1982.* Hantsport, N.S.: Lancelot Press, 1983.

Brox, Ottar. *Newfoundland Fishermen in the Age of Industry.* St. John's: Institute for Social and Economic Research, 1972.

Bryfogle, R. Charles. *City in Print: A Bibliography.* Agincourt, General Learning Press, 1974.

Brym, R.J. and R.J. Sacouman (eds.). *Underdevelopment and Social Movements in Atlantic Canada.* Toronto: New Hogtown Press, 1979.

Buckley, H. and E. Tihoranyi. "Canadian Politics for Rural Adjustment: A Summary of Conclusions." *Social and Cultural Change in Canada*, W.E. Mann (ed.). Toronto: Copp Clark, 1970.

Buckner, P.A. and David Frank (eds.). *Atlantic Canada After Confederation.* Fredericton: Acadiensis Press, 1988.

Buggey, Susan. "Building Halifax, 1841–1871." *Acadiensis* X, 1 (Autumn 1980): 90–122.

Burbridge, J.K. "The Atlantic Development Board and Atlantic Regional Development." M.A. Thesis, University of New Brunswick, 1971.

Burke, Chris D. *Holding the Line: A Strategy for Canada's Urban Development.* Ottawa: Ministry of State for Urban Affairs, 1976.

——. *An Urban/Economic Development Strategy for the Atlantic Region.* Toronto: Macmillan of Canada, 1976.

Burridge, Stephen, "Boosting the Maritimes: The Busy East, 1910–1925." M.A. Thesis, Carleton University, 1993.

Butler, A.M. *Halifax Relief Commission, 1918–1976.* Ottawa: Department of Finance, 1976.

Callum, C. "Rural Communities in Decline: The Newfoundland Experience." *Ekistics* (1976).

Cameron, James M. *Industrial History of the New Glasgow District.* New Glasgow, N.S.: Hector, 1963.

Cameron, Kenneth D. *National Urban Policy.* Ottawa: Town Planning Institute of Canada, 1972.

Cameron, S.D. "Charlottetown: Pleasures of a Small Town with the Stimulation of a City." *Canadian Geographic* (August–September 1984): 8–18.

Canadian National Railways, Department of Research and Development. *An Industrial Survey of Bathurst, New Brunswick.* Montreal: Canadian National Railway, 1960.

——. *An Industrial Survey of Dalhousie, New Brunswick.* Montreal: Canadian National Railway, 1962.

——. *An Industrial Survey of Greater Saint John, New Brunswick.* Montreal: Canadian National Railway, 1955

——. *An Industrial Survey of Lower Gloucester County, N.B.* Montreal: Canadian National Railway, 1962.

——. *An Industrial Survey of the Miramichi Area, Northumberland County, New Brunswick.* Montreal: Canadian National Railway, 1962.

——. *An Industrial Survey of Sydney, Nova Scotia*. Montreal: Canadian National Railway, 1959.

Canning, Stratford. "The Illusion of Progress: Rural Development Policy Since 1949." *Canadian Forum* 53, 6 (March 1974): 22–3.

Cannon, James. "Explaining Regional Development in Atlantic Canada: A Review Essay." *Journal of Canadian Studies* 19, 3 (1984): 65–86.

Careless, J.M.S. *Frontier and Metropolis: Regions, Cities and Identity in Canada Before 1914*. Toronto: University of Toronto Press, 1989.

——. "Aspects of Metropolitanism in Atlantic Canada." *Regionalism in the Canadian Community 1867–1967,* Mason Wade (ed.). Toronto: University of Toronto Press, 1969.

——. "Metropolis and Region: The Interplay Between City and Region Before 1914." *Urban History Review* 3 (1978): 99–118.

Carter, Harold. *An Introduction to Urban Historical Geography*. Baltimore: E. Arnold, 1983.

Castells, Manual. *The Urban Question: A Marxist Approach*. Cambridge, Mass.: Massachussettes Institute of Technology Press, 1977.

Central Mortgage and Housing Corporation. *Beyond Cynicism: Towards Communaute: A Report Jointly Appointed by the Central Mortgage and Housing Corporation and the Ministry of State for Urban Affairs*. Ottawa: 1972.

Charlottetown Centennial Committee. *Charlottetown Centennial 1855–1955*. Charlottetown: CTT, 1955.

Chisholm, Jessie. "Organizing On the Waterfront: The St. John's Longshoremen's Protective Union, 1890–1914." *Labour/Le Travail* 26 (Fall 1990): 37–59.

Clairmont, Donald H. and Dennis William Magill. *Africville: The Life and Death of a Canadian Black Community*. Revised edition. Toronto: Canadian Scholars' Press, 1987.

Clark, Andrew Hill. *Three Centuries and the Island: A Historical Geography of Settlement and Agriculture in Prince Edward Island*. Toronto: University of Toronto Press, 1959.

Clark, S.D. "The Rural Village Society of the Maritimes." *The Developing Community*. Toronto: University of Toronto Press, 1962.

Clow, Michael. "Politics and Uneven Capitalist Development: The Maritime Challenge to the Study of Canadian Political Economy." *Studies in Political Economy* 14 (Summer 1984): 117–40.

Coffey, William J. *Projections for Province, Counties and Halifax Metro Area*. Halifax: Dalhousie University, 1983.

Conrad, Margaret. "The Atlantic Revolution of the 1950s." *Beyond Anger and Longing: Community Development in Atlantic Canada*, Berkeley Fleming (ed.). Fredericton: 1988.

Copes, Parzival. *The Resettlement of Fishing Communities in Newfoundland*. Ottawa: Canadian Council on Rural Development. 1972.

——. *St. John's and Newfoundland: An Economic Survey*. St. John's: Newfoundland Board of Trade, 1961.

Couture, Yvon. *L'Acadie de Campbellton a Bathurst*. Rimouski: College de Rimouski, 1975.

Crawley, Ron. "Class Conflict and the Establishment of the Sydney Steel Industry, 1897–1904." *The Island: New Perspectives on Cape Breton's History, 1713–1990*. K.J. Donovan (ed.). Fredericton: Acadiensis Press, 1990.

——. "Off to Sydney: Newfoundlanders Emigrate to Industrial Cape Breton, 1890–1914." *Acadiensis* XVII, 2 (Spring 1988): 27–51.

Cruikshank, Ken. *Close Ties: Railways, Government and the Board of Railway Commissioners, 1851–1933*. Montreal: McGill-Queens University Press, 1991.

——. "The Intercolonial Railway, Freight Rates and the Maritime Economy." *Acadiensis* XXII, 1 (Autumn 1992): 87–110.

——."The People's Railway: The Intercolonial Railway and the Canadian Public Enterprise Experience." *Acadiensis* XVI, 1 (Autumn 1986): 58–77.

Dahms, Fred A. "The Process of 'Urbanization' in the Countryside: A Study of Huron and Bruce Counties, 1891–1981." *Urban History Review* (February 1984): 1–18.

Dalhousie Genealogical Society. *Restigouche County History*. Dalhousie: Restigouche Regional Museum, May 1987.

Davis, Anthony. "Organization of Production and Market Relations in a Nova Scotian Inshore Fishing Community." *Papers in Anthropology*. Winnipeg: University of Manitoba, 1975.

Davis, J.M. "Considerations in the Investigation, Analysis and Planning of the Central Areas of Maritime Cities." *Issues in Regional/Urban Development of Atlantic Canada*. Saint John: University of New Brunswick, 1978.

DeLottinville, Peter. "The St. Croix Cotton Manufacturing Company and Its Influence on the St. Crois Community, 1880–1892." M.A. Thesis, Dalhousie University, 1979.

——. "Trouble in the Hives of Industry: The Cotton Industry Comes to Milltown, New Brunswick, 1879–1892." *Canadian Historical Association Historical Papers*. 1980.

Department of Development (Nova Scotia). *Industrial Cape Breton Fact Book*. Third edition. September 1984.

Department of Industry, Trade and Technology (Nova Scotia). *Halifax Metro Area Fact Book*. Seventh edition. Halifax: 1988.

——. *Nova Scotia Statistical Review*. Sixth edition. Halifax: 1989.

Dewar, W.Y. *Urban Canada*. Don Mills, Ont.: J.M. Dent and Sons, 1972.

DREE. *Climate for Development: Atlantic Region*. Working paper prepared for submission to the Standing Committee on Regional Development. 1976.

——. *Economic Development Prospects in Nova Scotia*. 1979.

——. *Living Together: A Study of Regional Disparities*. Ottawa: Supply and Services Canada, 1977.

——. *Newfoundland: From Dependency to Self-Reliance*. Ottawa: Supply and Services Canada, 1980.

Erickson, Paul A. *Halifax's North End*. Hantsport, N.S.: Lancelot Press, 1986.

Fairley, Bryant "The Struggle for Capitalism in the Fishing Industry of Newfoundland." *Studies in Political Economy* 17 (Summer 1985): 33–70.

Fairly, Bryant, Colin Leys and James Sacouman (eds.). *Restructuring and Resistance From Atlantic Canada*. Toronto: Garamond Press, 1990.

Fingard, Judith. *The Dark Side of Life in Victorian Halifax*. Porters Lake, N.S.: Pottersfield Press, 1989.

——. "The Decline of the Sailor as a Ship Labourer in 19th-Century Timber Ports." *Labour/Le Travail* 2 (1977): 35–53.

——. "Masters and Friends, Crimps and Abstainers: Agents of Control in 19th Century Sailortown." *Acadiensis* VIII, 1 (Autumn 1978): 22–46.

——. "The Relief of the Unemployed Poor in Saint John, Halifax and St. John's, 1815–1860." *Acadiensis* V, 1 (Autumn 1975): 32–53.

Fischer, Lewis R. and Eric W. Sager (eds.). *The Enterprising Canadians: Entrepreneurs and Economic Development in Eastern Canada, 1820–1914*. St. John's: Memorial University, 1976.

Fleming, Berkeley. *Beyond Anger and Longing: Community Development in Atlantic Canada*. Fredericton: Acadiensis Press, 1988.

Fleming, Susan. "The Growth-Centre Concept: Its Application in the Maritime Provinces." M.A. Thesis, University of New Brunswick, 1979.

Fletcher, R.K. *Post-War Agriculture Trends in the Atlantic Provinces*. Research Paper No. 3. Halifax: Atlantic Provinces Economic Council, 1966.

Foote, R.L. *The Case of Port Hawkesbury: Rapid Industrialization and Social Unrest in a Nova Scotia Community*. Toronto: Peter Martin Associates Books, 1979.

Forbes, Ernest R. *Challenging the Regional Stereotype*. Fredericton: Acadiensis Press, 1989.

——. *The Maritime Rights Movement 1919–1927*. Montreal: McGill-Queen's University Press, 1979.

——. "Never the Twain Shall Meet: Prairie-Maritime Relations, 1910–1927." *Canadian Historical Review* LIX (March 1978).

Forbes, E.R. and D.A. Muise (eds.). *Atlantic Canada in Confederation*. Toronto: University of Toronto Press, 1993.

Forward, C.N. "Cities: Function, Form and Future." *Studies in Canadian Geography: The Atlantic Provinces,* Alan MacPherson (ed.). Toronto: University of Toronto Press, 1972.

——. "Parallelism of Halifax and Victoria." *Canadian Geographical Journal* (March 1975): 34–43.

——. "Recent Changes in the Form and Function of the Port of St. John's, Newfoundland." *Canadian Geographer* 11, 2 (1967): 101–16.

Frank, David. "The Cape Breton Coal Industry and the Rise and Fall of the British Empire Steel Corporation." *Acadiensis* VII, 1 (Autumn 1977): 3–34.

——. "Class Conflict in the Coal Industry: Cape Breton 1922." *Essays in Canadian Working Class History,* Gregory Kealey and Peter Warrian (eds.). Toronto: McClelland and Stewart, 1976.

——. "Coal Masters and Coal Miners: The 1922 Strike and the Roots of Class Conflict in the Cape Breton Coal Industry." M.A. Thesis, Dalhousie University, 1974.

——. "Company Town/Labour Town: Local Government in the Cape Breton Coal Towns, 1917–1926." *Histoire sociale/Social History* XIV, 27 (May 1981): 177–196.

——. "Contested Terrain: Workers' Control in Cape Breton Coal Mines." *On the Job,* Craig Heron and Storey (eds.). Kingston: McGill-Queen's University Press, 1986.

——. "Tradition and Culture in the Cape Breton Mining Community in the Early Twentieth Century." *Cape Breton at 200: Historical Essays in Honour of the Island's Bicentennial, 1785–1985,* Kenneth Donovan (ed.). Sydney, N.S.: University College of Cape Breton Press, 1985.

Freeman, Milton M.R. (ed.). *Intermediate Adaptation in Newfoundland and the Arctic: A Strategy of Social and Economic Development*. St. John's: Institute for Social and Economic Research, 1969.

Frost, J.D. "The 'Nationalization' of the Bank of Nova Scotia, 1880–1910." *Industrialization and Underdevelopment in the Maritimes, 1880–1930,* T.W. Acheson, D. Frank and J.D. Frost. Toronto: Garamond Press, 1985.

Frost, James. "Principles of Interest: The Bank of Nova Scotia and the Industrialization of the Maritimes 1880–1910." M.A. Thesis, Queen's University, 1979.

Garland, R.E. "Government Centralization in New Brunswick." *Issues in Regional/Urban Development of Atlantic Canada,* Neil Ridler (ed.). Social Science Monograph Series Vol. II. Saint John: Spring, 1978.

Gertler, Leonard O. and Ronald W. Crowley. *Changing Canadian Cities: The Next 25 Years.* Ministry of State for Urban Affairs. Toronto: McClelland and Stewart, Ltd., 1977.

George, Roy E. "The Cape Breton Development Corporation." *Public Corporations and Public Policy in Canada*, A. Tupper and G.B. Doern (eds.). Montreal: Institute for Research of Public Policy, 1981.

——. *A Leader and a Laggard: Manufacturing Industry in Nova Scotia, Quebec and Ontario.* Toronto: University of Toronto Press, 1970.

Gierman, D.M. *Rural to Urban Land Conversion.* Ottawa: Environment Canada, Lands Directorate, 1980.

Goracz, Albert B. *The Urban Future.* Ottawa: Central Mortgage and Housing Corporation, 1971.

Gore, Charles. *Regions in Question: Space, Development Theory and Regional Policy.* London: Methuen, 1984.

Gosse, John S.R. *Whitbourne, Newfoundland's First Inland Town: Journey Back in Time.* Whitbourne: the author, 1985.

Graham, John F. "Economic Development of the Atlantic Provinces." *The Dalhousie Review* XI, 1 (Spring 1960): 50–60.

——. *Provincial-Municipal Relations in the Maritime Provinces.* Fredericton: Maritime Union Study, 1970.

Grant, J.W. "Population Shifts in the Maritimes." *Dalhousie Review* 18, 3 (October 1937): 282–94.

Guy, R.M. "Industrial Development and the urbanization of Pictou County, Nova Scotia to 1900." M.A. Thesis, Acadia University, 1962.

Hackson, John N. *The Canadian City: Space, Form, Quality.* Toronto: McGraw-Hill Ryerson Ltd., 1973.

Hamer, D.A. *New Towns in the New World: Images and Perceptions of the Nineteenth-Century Urban Frontier.* New York: Columbia University Press, 1990.

Hanson, Arthur, Leonard Kasden and Cynthia Lamson. "Atlantic Coastal Communities: Problems and Prospects." *Atlantic Fisheries and Coastal Communities,* C. Lamson and A.Hanson (eds.). Halifax: Ocean Studies Program, Dalhousie University, 1984.

Harnett, Ken O. *Encounter on Urban Environment: Historian's Report.* Halifax: Voluntary Economic Planning Board, 1970.

Harris, R.C. "Historical Geography in Canada." *Canadian Geographer* 11, 4 (1967).

Harvey, Andrew S. *The Export Base of the Pictou County Economy.* Halifax: Dalhousie University, Institute of Public Affairs, 1968.

——. *Pictou County Housing Capability.* Halifax: Dalhousie University, Institute of Public Affairs, 1970.

Harvey, D.C. "Charlottetown." *Canadian Geographical Journal* (April 1932): 200–19.

Harvey, Edmund Roy. *Sydney, Nova Scotia: An Urban Study.* Toronto: Clarke Irwin, 1971.

Hazelton, R. "Labour in Prince Edward Island: A Case Study." *Labour in Atlantic Canada,* R. Chanteloup (ed.). St. John: University of New Brunswick Press, 1981.

Hefferton, S.J. "Planning for Small Towns in Newfoundland." *Community Planning Review* (March 1958): 11–15.

Henderson, George Fletcher. *Federal Royal Commissions in Canada, 1867–1966: A Checklist.* Toronto: University of Toronto Press, 1967.

Hensen, G. "A Regional City Plans its Future." *Community Planning Review* 11, 1 (1961): 13–26.

Higgins, Donald J.H. "Canada: New Brunswick and Nova Scotia." *International Handbook on Local Government Reorganization: Contemporary Developments,* D.C. Rowat (ed.). Westport, Conn.: Greenwood Press, 1980.

——. *Local and Urban Politics in Canada.* Toronto: Gage Publishing, 1986.

Higgins, D.J.H. and Linda Christiansen-Ruffman. "Halifax-Dartmouth: The Politics of Public Waterfront Development." *City Magazine* (October 1977): 37–51.

Hiller, James. "The Origins of the Pulp and Paper Industry in Newfoundland." *Acadiensis* XI, 2 (Spring 1982): 42–68.

——. "The Politics of Newsprint: The Newfoundland Pulp and Paper Industry, 1915–1939." *Acadiensis* XIX, 2 (Spring 1990): 3–39.

Hiller, James and Peter Neary (eds.). *Newfoundland in the Nineteenth and Twentieth Centuries: Essays in Interpretation.* Toronto: University of Toronto Press, 1980.

Hilton, Keith David. *The Iron Mining Communities of Quebec-Labrador: A Study of a Resource Frontier.* Ottawa, 1968.

Hodge, Gerald. "Canadian Small Town Renaissance: Implications for Settlement System Concepts." *Regional Studies* 17, 1 (February 1983): 19–28.

——. *Rural and Urban Development Capability in Prince Edward Island.* Toronto: Acres Research and Planning, 1967.

——. "Urban Structure and Regional Development." *Regional Science Association Papers.* 1968.

Hoggart, K. "Resettlement in Newfoundland." *Geography* 64, 3 (1979). 215–18.

Hooper, Diana. *The Changing Economic Basis of Canadian Urban Growth, 1971–81.* Toronto: Centre for Urban and Community Studies, University of Toronto, 1983.

Hoover, Dwight W. *Cities.* New York: R.R. Bowker and Co., 1976.

Hornsby, Stephen. *Nineteenth Century Cape Breton: A Historical Geography.* Montreal: McGill-Queens University Press, 1992.

Horwood, Harold. *Cornerbrook: A Social History of a Paper Town.* St. John's: Breakwater Books, 1986.

Howell, Colin D. "Baseball, Class and Community in the Maritime Provinces, 1870–1910." *Histoire sociale/Social History* XXII, 44 (November 1989): 265–86.

Howland, R.D. *Some Regional Aspects of Canada's Economic Development.* A study prepared for the Royal Commission on Canada's Economic Prospects. Ottawa: 1957.

Hymer, Stephen. "The Multinational Corporation and the Law of Uneven Development." *International Firms and Modern Imperialism,* H. Radice (ed.). Harmondsworth: Penguin, 1975.

Jackson, Elva E. *Windows on the Past: North Sydney, Nova Scotia.* Windsor, N.S.: Lancelot Press, 1974.

Jackson, John N. *The Canadian City: Space, Form, Quality*. Toronto: McGraw-Hill Ryerson, 1973.

Jenson, L.B. *Country Roads: Rural Pictou County*. Halifax: Petheric Press, 1974.

Jobb, Dean. "The Politics of the New Brunswick and Prince Edward Railway, 1872–1886." *Acadiensis* XIII, 2 (Spring 1984): 69–90.

Johnson, Catherine E. "The Search for Industry in Newcastle, New Brunswick, 1899–1914." *Acadiensis* XIII, 1 (Autumn 1983): 93–111.

Johnson, H. Thomas. *Urbanization and Economic Growth in Canada: 1851–1971*. London: University of Western Ontario Press, 1973.

——. *Urban Settlement Distribution: The Dynamics of Canada's System*. Vancouver: Centre for Human Settlements, Faculty of Graduate Studies, University of British Columbia, 1987.

Johnson, Peter Graham. "The Union of Nova Scotia Municipalities as a Pressure Group." M.A. Thesis, Dalhousie University, 1967.

Jones, Kenneth. "Response to Regional Disparity in the Maritime Provinces, 1926–1942: A Study in Canadian Intergovernmental Relations." M.A. Thesis, University of New Brunswick, 1980.

Kahn, Alison Joanne. *Listen While I Tell You: A Story of the Jews of St. John's Newfoundland*. St. John's: Memorial University, 1987.

Keats, Peat, Marwick and Company. *Public Transit: Halifax; A Study of the Basic Components of Public Transit in the City of Halifax and their Improvement*. Toronto: Halifax Transit Commission, 1970.

Kennedy, Leslie. *The Urban Kaleidoscope: Canadian Perspectives*. Toronto: McGraw-Hill Ryerson, 1983.

Kennedy, Sean M. *Final Report on Urbanization in Canada*. Ottawa: Canada Post, Environmental Forecasting, Marketing Services Branch, 1975.

Kensington Lion's Club. *The History of Kensington: It Includes the Story of the Town of Kensington Up to and Including Centennial Year 1973*. Kensington: Lion's Club, 1973.

Kent, Tom. "The Brief Rise and Early Decline of Regional Development." *Acadiensis* IX, 1 (Autumn 1979): 120–125

Kerans, Pat. "Bad News for Atlantic Canada." *Perception* 9, 3 (1986): 14–16.

Kerr, Donald and Deryck Holdsworth (eds.). *Historical Atlas of Canada, Vol. III. Addressing the Twentieth Century*. Toronto: University of Toronto Press, 1990.

Krueger, Ralph and John Koegler. *Regional Development in Northeast New Brunswick*. Toronto: 1975.

Lamson, C. and A. Hanson (eds.). *Atlantic Fisheries and Coastal Communities*. Halifax: Ocean Studies Program, Dalhousie University, 1984.

Lang, Nicole. "L'impact d'une industrie: Les effets sociaux de l'arrivée de la compagnie Fraser Limited à Edmundston, N.-B., 1900–1950." *Revue de la Société historique de Madawaska* XV, 1–2 (Jan–Juin, 1987).

Lang, V. "Land Use Problems and Priorities in the Fringes of St. John's, Newfoundland." *Urban Forum* (Summer 1976): 12–15.

Langhout, Rosemary. "Developing Nova Scotia: Railways and Public Accounts, 1848–1867." *Acadiensis* XVI, 2 (Spring 1985): 3–28.

Latimer, J.H. "Agriculture." *The Economic Effects of the War on the Maritime Provinces of Canada*, B.S. Kierstead (ed.). Halifax: Dalhousie University, Institute of Public Affairs, 1944.

Latremouille, J. *Pride of Home: The Working Class Housing Tradition of Nova Scotia, 1749–1949*. Hantsport, N.S.: Lancelot Press, 1986.

Lawson, M.J. *History of the Townships of Dartmouth, Preston and Lawrencetown, Halifax County, N.S.* Belleville, Ont.: Mika, 1972.

Leblanc, Phyllis. "Moncton, 1870–1937: A Community in Transition." Unpublished Ph.D. Thesis, University of Ottawa, 1988.

Leefe, J. Ed. "Sydney Morton's Diary." Document. *Acadiensis* IV, 1 (Autumn 1974): 121–29.

Leger, Lauraine. *Les sanctions popularies en Acadie, region du comte de Kent.* Montreal: Lemeac, 1978.

Levitt, Kari. *Population Movements in Atlantic Canada.* Halifax: Atlantic Provinces Economic Council, 1960.

Lewis, Jane and Mark Shrimpton. "Policymaking in Newfoundland During the 1940s: The Case of the St. John's Housing Corporation." *Canadian Historical Review* LXV (June 1984): 209–39.

Libick, Helma. *A Bibliography of Canadian Thesis and Dissertations in Urban, Regional and Environmental Planning, 1974–1979.* Montreal: Canadian Association of Political Scientists, Bibliography Committee, 1980.

Lithwick, N.H. *Regional Economic Policy: the Canadian Experience.* Toronto: McGraw-Hill Ryerson, 1978.

——. *Urban Canada: Problems and Prospects.* Ottawa: Central Mortgage and Housing Corporation, 1970.

Lounsbury, F.E. *Secondary Manufacturing in the Atlantic Provinces.* Halifax: Atlantic Provinces Economic Council, 1961.

MacBeath, George B. *The Story of the Restigouche: Covering the Indians, French and English Periods of the Restigouche Area.* Saint John: The New Brunswick Museum, 1954.

MacCallum, Margaret E. "Separate Spheres: The Organization of Work in a Confectionary Factory: Ganong Bros., St. Stephen, New Brunswick." *Labour/Le Travail* 24 (Autumn 1989): 69–90.

Macgillivray, Don. "Henry Melville Whitney Comes to Cape Breton: The Saga of a Gilded Age Entrepreneur." *Acadiensis* IX, 1 (Autumn 1979): 135–82.

Macgillivray, Don and Brian Tennyson (eds.). *Cape Breton Historical Essays.* Sydney: College of Cape Breton Press, 1980.

Machum, L.A. *A History of Moncton, Town and City, 1855–1965.* Moncton: City of Moncton, 1965.

MacKay, Carole. "Canadian Regionalism: The Atlantic Development Board: A Case Study." M.A. Thesis, McGill University, 1969.

MacKay, Ian. "Strikes in the Maritimes, 1901–1914." *Atlantic Canada After Confederation,* P.A. Buckner and David Frank (eds.). Fredericton: Acadiensis Press, 1988.

MacKay, R. (ed.). *Newfoundland: Economic, Diplomatic, and Strategic Studies.* Toronto: Oxford University Press, 1946.

MacKinnon, D.A. and A.B. Warburton (eds.). *Past and Present of Prince Edward Island: Embracing Concise Review of its Early Settlement, Development and Present Conditions.* Charlottetown: B.F. Brown, 1906.

MacKinnon, Frank. "Charlottetown's Centennial." *Canadian Geographical Journal* (July 1955): 238–43.

MacKinnon, J.G. *Old Sydney: Sketches of the Town and its People in the Days Gone By.* Belleville, Ont.: Mika, 1973.

MacKinnon, Richard. "Carriage Making in St. John's, Newfoundland: A Folkloristic Perspective on a Historical Industry." *Material History Review* 27 (Spring 1988): 1–13.

MacKinnon, Robert. "Farming the Rock: The Evolution of Commercial Agriculture around St. John's Newfoundland to 1945." *Acadiensis* XX, 2 (Spring 1991): 32–61.

MacKinnon, W.E. "The Politics of Planning: A Case Study of the P.E.I. Development Plan." M.A. Thesis, Dalhousie, 1978.

Maclaren, Virginia. *Sustainable Urban Development in Canada: From Concept to Practise*. Toronto: Institute for Community, Urban and Regional Research Press, 1992.

MacLeod, Ada. *Road to Summerside: The Story of Early Summerside and the Surrounding area*. Summerside: the author, 1980.

MacOwan, Brian H. "The Evolution of a Regional Urban Network: New Brunswick and Nova Scotia, 1871–1971." Ph.D. Thesis, University of Waterloo, 1986.

MacLeod, Malcolm. *Peace of the Continent: The Impact of Second World War Canadian and American Bases in Newfoundland*. St. John's: Creative Printers and Publishers, 1986.

MacQuarrie, Marjorie Elaine. "Geographic Effects of Heritage Area Conservation Upon Three Canadian Cities." Undergraduate thesis, Carleton University, 1979.

Mann, O. Nelson. "Atlantic Provinces Economic Council." *Dalhousie Review* 35, No. 4 (Winter 1956): 309–22.

——. "An Overall Planning Scheme is a Must for the Atlantic Provinces." *Financial Times* (9 November 1964).

Mansell, Robert and Lawrence Copithorne. "Canadian Regional Economic Disparities: A Survey." *Disparities and Interregional Adjustment*, K. Norrie (ed.). Toronto: University of Toronto Press, 1984.

Maritime Union Study (Deutsch Commission). Report on Maritime Union commissioned by the Governments of Nova Scotia, New Brunswick and Prince Edward Island. 1970.

Matthews, Ralph. "Canadian Regional Development Strategy: A Dependency Theory Perspective." *Plan Canada* 17, No. 2 (1977): 131–43.

——. *The Creation of Regional Dependency*. Toronto: University of Toronto Press, 1983.

——. "The Pursuit of Progress: Newfoundland's Social and Economic Development in the Smallwood Era." *Issues in the Regional/Urban Development of Atlantic Canada*, Neil B. Ridler (ed.). Social Science Monograph Series, Vol. 2 (Spring 1978).

——. "The Smallwood Legacy: The Development of Underdevelopment in Newfoundland, 1949–1972." *Journal of Canadian Studies* 13, No. 4 (1979): 89–108.

——. *'There's No Better Place Than Here': Social Change in Three Newfoundland Outports*. Toronto: Peter Martin, 1976.

Matthews, Ralph and Noel Iverson. *Communities in Decline: An Examination of Household Resettlement in Newfoundland*. St. John's: 1968.

Maxwell, L.M.B. *The History of Central New Brunswick*. Sackville: 1937.

McAllister, R.L. "Canadian Program Experiences." *Regional Economic Policy: The Canadian Experience*, Harvey Lithwick (ed.). Toronto: McGraw-Hill, 1978.

McCalla, Robert J. "Separation and Specialization of Land Uses in City Port Waterfronts: The Cases of St. John and Halifax." *Canadian Geographer* XXVII (1983): 48–61.

McCann, L.D. "Halifax: Centre at the Edge." *Horizon Canada*. 1985.

——. "The Mercantile-Industrial Transition in the Metal Towns of Pictou County, 1857–1931." *Acadiensis* X, 2 (Spring 1981): 29–64.

——. "Metropolitanism and Branch Businesses in the Maritimes, 1881–1931." *Acadiensis* XIII, 1 (Autumn 1983): 112–25.

——. "Staples and the New Industrialism in the Growth of Post-Confederation Halifax." *Acadiensis* VIII, 2 (Spring 1979): 47–80.

McCann, L.D. (ed.). *People and Place: Studies of Small Town Life in the Maritimes.* Fredericton: 1988.

McCay, Bonnie J. "'Fish is Scarce': Fisheries Modernization Fogo Island, Newfoundland." *North Atlantic Maritime Cultures: Anthropological Essays on Changing Adaptations*. The Hague: Mouton, 1979.

McClellan, John. "Changing Patterns of Land Use." *The Garden Transformed: Prince Edward Island 1945–1980,* V. Smitheram, D. Milne and S. Dasgupta (eds.). Charlottetown: Ragweed Press, 1982.

McFarland, Joan. "Changing Modes of Social Control in a Fish Packing Town." *Studies in Political Economy* 4 (1980): 99–113.

McGahan, Elizabeth. *The Port of Saint John. Vol. I.* Ottawa: National Harbours Board, 1982.

McGahan, Peter. *Police Images of a City.* New York: Lang, 1984.

——. *Urban Sociology in Canada.* Toronto: Butterworths, 1982.

McKay, Ian. "The Crisis of Dependent Development: Class Conflict in the Nova Scotia Coalfields, 1872–76." *Class, Gender and Region: Essays in Canadian Historical Sociology,* Greg Keale. (ed.). St. John's: Committee on Canadian Labour History, 1988.

——. "Industry, Work and Community in the Cumberland Coalfields, 1848–1927." Ph.D. Dissertation, Dalhousie University, 1983.

——. "The Realm of Uncertainty: The Experience of Work in the Cumberland Coal Mines, 1873–1927." *Acadiensis* XXVI, 1 (Autumn 1986): 3–57.

——. "Springhill, 1958." *New Maritimes* (December 1983–January 1984).

——. "Strikes in the Maritimes, 1901–1914." *Acadiensis* (Autumn 1983): 3–45.

——. "The Working Class of Metropolitan Halifax, 1850–1899." B.A. Hons. Essay, Dalhousie University, 1975.

McNabb, Debra. *Old Sydney Town: historic buildings of the north end, 1785 to 1938.* Sydney, N.S.: Old Sydney Society, 1986.

Meacham, J.H. & Co. *Illustrated Historical Atlas of the Province of Prince Edward Island 1880. Centennial '73* Commemorative Edition. Belleville, Ont.: Mika, 1973.

Mensah, Ernest. "The Demographic and Ecological Perspectives of Spatial Distribution in Fredericton and Saint John, 1971–1976." M.A. Thesis, University of New Brunswick, 1982.

Miller, M.H. *History of Upper Woodstock.* Saint John: 1940.

Mills, J.R. "Voluntary Economic Planning in Nova Scotia." *Canadian Public Administration* 8, No. 2 (June 1965): 160–5.

Millward, Hugh. *The Geography of Housing in Metropolitan Halifax, Nova Scotia.* Atlantic Region Geographical Studies #3. Halifax: Saint Mary's University, 1981.

Ministry of State for Urban Affairs. *Annual Report, 1971/72 to 1978/79.*

Ministry of State for Urban Affairs. *Le Canada urbain: Hier, aujourd'hui et demain.* Ottawa: 1975.

Momatiuk, Yva and John Eastcott. *This Marvellous Terrible Place: Images of New-foundland and Labrador*. Camden East: Camden House, 1988.

Morley, William F.E. *The Atlantic Provinces*. Vol. 1 of *Canadian Local Histories: A Bibliography*. Toronto: University of Toronto Press, 1967.

Morton, Suzanne. "The Halifax Relief Commission and Labour Relations during the Reconstruction of Halifax, 1917–1915." *Acadiensis* XVIII, 2 (Spring 1989): 73–93.

Muise, Del. "'The Great Transformation': Changing the Urban Face of Nova Scotia, 1871–1921." *Nova Scotia Historical Review* (Autumn 1991): 1–27.

——. "The Industrial Context of Inequality: Female Participation in Nova Scotia's Paid Labour Force, 1871–1921." *Acadiensis* XX (Spring 1991).

——. "The Making of an Industrial Community: Cape Breton's Coal Towns, 1867–1900." *Cape Breton Historical Essays*, Don MacGillivray and Brian Tennyson (eds.). Sydney: 1980.

Munske, R.R. "Development of the Urban System in Newfoundland." M.A. Thesis, George Washington University, 1974.

Murphy, J. Elmer. *A Newspaperman Remembers: Tales of Thirty-eight Years of Newspaper Work and Other Reminiscences*. Summerside: 1980.

Murphy, Thomas R. "From Family Farming to Capitalist Agriculture: Food Production, Agribusiness, and the State." *Restructuring and Resistance: Perspectives from Atlantic Canada*, Bryant Fairley, Colin Leys and James Sacouman (eds.). Toronto: Garamond, 1990.

Neary, Peter *Newfoundland in the North Atlantic World, 1929–1949*. Montreal: McGill-Queen's University Press, 1988.

——. *The Political Economy of Newfoundland, 1929–1972*. Toronto: Copp Clark, 1973.

——. "'Traditional' and 'Modern' Elements in the Social and Economic History of Bell Island and Conception Bay." *Canadian Historical Association Historical Papers* (1973): 105–36.

Neis, Barbara. "Competitive Merchants and Class Struggle in Newfoundland." *Studies in Political Economy* 5 (Spring 1981): 127–43.

Nemetz, Donald. "Managing Development." *The Garden Transformed: Prince Edward Island 1945–1980*, V. Smitheram, D. Milne and S. Dasgupta (eds.). Charlottetown: Ragweed Press, 1982.

Newton, D. "What is Happening in Cape Breton?" *Canadian Geographical Journal* 87, No. 5 (November 1973): 24–31.

Novack, Jack (ed.). *A Guide to Local Government in Prince Edward Island*. Halifax: MMTDB, 1984.

Oberlander, H.P. and Arthur L. Fallick (eds.). *The Ministry of State for Urban Affairs: A Courageous Experiment in Public Administration*. Vancouver: Centre for Human Settlements, Faculty of Graduate Studies, University of British Columbia, 1987.

Ommer, Rosemary (ed.). *Merchant Credit and Labour Strategies in Historical Perspective*. Fredericton: 1990.

O'Neil, Paul. *Oldest City: The Story of St. John's, Newfoundland*. Erin, Ont.: Press Porcepic, 1975.

——. *Seaport Legacy of St. John's*. Erin, Ont.: Press Porcepic, 1976.

O'Neill, T.J. *Educator, Advocate and Critic, Atlantic Provinces Economic Council 25 Years*. Halifax: Atlantic Provinces Economic Council, 1979.

Overton, James. "Oil and Gas: The Rhetoric and Reality of Development in Newfoundland." *Contrary Winds: Essays on Newfoundland Society in Crisis*. St. John's: Breakwater Books, 1986.

——. "Riots, Raids, and Relief, Police, Prisons and Parsimony: The Political
    Economy of Public Order in Newfoundland in the 1930s." *Violence and
    Popular Anxiety: A Canadian Case,* E. Leyton, W. O'Grady and J. Overton
    (eds.).

——. "Progressive Conservatism? A Critical Look at Politics, Culture and Devel-
    opment in Newfoundland." *Ethnicity in Atlantic Canada,* Social Mono-
    graph Series, Vol. 5, 1985.

——. "Uneven Development in Canada: The Case of Newfoundland." *Review of
    Radical Political Economics* 10, No. 3 (1978): 106–16.

Overton, James and Lee Seymour. "Towards Understanding Rural Social
    Change: A Critique of *There's No Better Place Than Here." Our Generation* 12,
    No. 1 (1977).

Pacey, Elizabeth. *The Battle of Citadel Hill.* Hantsport, N.S.: Lancelot Press,
    1979.

Paine, R.P.B., M.L. Skolnik and C. Wadel. "Intermediate Adaptation – Rural
    Development as an Alternative to Rural Immiseration." *Intermediate Adap-
    tation in Newfoundland and the Artic,* M.M.R. Freeman (ed.). St. John's:
    Institute for Social and Economic Research, 1969.

Paris, Jacques and Gerald Hodge. *The System of Central Places in P.E.I..* Toronto:
    Acres Research and Planning, 1967.

Parks, A.C. *The Economy of the Atlantic Provinces 1940–1958.* Halifax: Atlantic
    Provinces Economic Council, 1960.

Patterson, George D.D. *History of the County of Pictou.* James M'Lean and Co.,
    1877.

Payn, E. "An Industrial Revolution for Cape Breton." *Atlantic Advocate* 60, No.
    1 (September 1969): 29–33.

Payzant, Joan *Halifax: Cornerstone of Canada.* Burlington: Windsor Publica-
    tions, 1985.

Pearson, Norman. *Town of Glace Bay, Nova Scotia, Urban Renewal Study.* 1966.

——. *Town of Windsor, Nova Scotia: Urban Renewal Study.*

People's Commission on Unemployment. *'Now That We've Burned Our Boats'.*
    St. John's: Newfoundland and Labrador Federation of Labour, 1978.

Pepin, Pierre-Yves. *Life and Poverty in the Maritimes.* Ottawa: Agricultural
    Research and Development Agency, 1968.

Peterson, Roger. "Transportation and Development in Atlantic Canada." *Issues
    in Regional/Urban Development of Atlantic Canada,* N.B. Ridler (ed.). Saint
    John: University of New Brunswick, 1978.

Philbrook, T.V. *Fisherman, Logger, Merchant, Miner: Social Change and Industrial-
    ism in Three Newfoundland Communities.* St. John's: Institute for Social and
    Economic Studies, Memorial University, 1966.

Phillips, Paul. *Regional Disparities.* Toronto: James Lorimer and Co. 1978.

Plunkett, Thomas J. *Understanding Urban Development in Canada.* Toronto:
    Canadian Foundation for Economic Education, 1977.

Poetschke, L.E. and T. Shovciw. "Activity Status Report – Regional Communi-
    ties Development: Managing the Development Process, Newfoundland
    and Labrador." Canada, Department of Regional Economic Expansion,
    contract Number 2106, 1974.

Porter, Helen. *Below the Bridge: Memories of the South Side of St. John's.* St. John's:
    Breakwater, 1979.

Powell, C.W. *St. John's Urban Region: Feasibility Report on Boundary and Structural
    Changes for Local Government in the Urban Core Area.* St. John's: Dept. of
    Municipal Affairs, 1981.

Pressman, Norman and Kathleen Lauder. "Resource Towns as New Towns."
    Urban History Review 1 (1978): 78–95.
Prince, S.H. *Catastrophe and Social Change: Based Upon a Sociological Study of the*
    Halifax Disaster. New York: Columbia University, Longmans, Green &
    Co., 1920.
Prince Edward Island Department of Industry and Commerce. Industrial Intel-
    ligence Unit. *A Community Profile of Summerside.* Charlottetown: 1973.
——. *A Community Profile of Charlottetown.* Charlottetown: 1973.
Pross, A. Paul. *Planning and Development: A Case of Two Nova Scotia Communi-*
    ties. Halifax: Institute of Public Affairs, 1975.
——. "The Role of Provincial Government in Development Planning: The Case
    of Two Nova Scotia Communities [Port Hawkesbury and Bridgewater]."
    Urban Forum (Winter 1975–76): 17–20.
Rankin, Robert Allan. *Down at the Shore: A History of Summerside, P.E.I.*
    1752–1945. Charlottetown: Prince Edward Island Heritage Foundation,
    1980.
Ray, D.M. "Dimensions of Canadian Regionalism." Geographical Paper No.
    49. Ottawa: Department of Energy, Mines and Resources, 1971.
——. "The Location of U.S. Manufacturing Subsidiaries in Canada." *Canadian*
    Economic Geography 47 (1971): 389–400.
Rees, R. "Changing Saint John: The Old and the New." *Canadian Geographical*
    Journal (May 1975): 12–17."
Reilly, Nolan. "The Emergence of Class Consciousness in Industrial Nova Sco-
    tia: A Case Study of Amherst, 1881–1925." Ph.D. Thesis, Dalhousie Uni-
    versity, 1982.
——. "The General Strike in Amherst, 1919." *Acadiensis* IX, 2 (Spring 1980):
    56–77.
Renouf, Harold A. *Financial Situation of Certain Depressed Municipalities: West-*
    ville, Dominion, New Waterford, Nova Scotia. Halifax: Dalhousie University,
    1964.
Report of the Task Group on the Proposed Closure of CFB Summerside. Summerside:
    Task Group on the Proposed Closure of CFB, 1989.
Rider, Peter. "Charlottetown: Mini-Metropolis." *Horizon Canada.* 1985.
Roberts, Ellis Noel Rees. *The Residential Desirability of Canadian Cities.* Toronto:
    1974.
Robinson, Ira M. *Canadian Urban Growth Trends: Implications for a National Set-*
    tlement Policy. Vancouver: University of British Columbia Press, 1981.
Robinson, Ira M. *New Industrial Towns on Canada's Resource Frontier.* Chicago:
    University of Chicago Press, 1962.
Rogers, Irene L. *Charlottetown: The Life in Its Buildings.* Charlottetown: Prince
    Edward Island Museum and Heritage Foundation, 1983.
Roper, Henry. "The Halifax Board of Control: The Failure of Municipal
    Reform, 1906–1919." *Acadiensis* XIV, 2 (Spring 1985): 46–65.
Rowat, D.C. *Halifax: A Case for a Metropolitan Authority.* Limited circulation
    report: 1949.
——. *Reorganization of Provincial-Municipal Relations in Nova Scotia.* Halifax:
    Nova Scotia Department of Municipal Affairs, 1949.
Rowe, Frederick W. *A History of Newfoundland and Labrador.* Toronto: McGraw-
    Hill-Ryerson, 1980.
Royal Commission on Canada's Economic Prospects (Gordon Commission).
    Report. 1957.

Royal Commission on Canada's Economic Prospects (Gordon Commission). *Submission of the Government of Nova Scotia*. October 1955.

Royal Commission on Dominion-Provincial Relations. *Report*. 1938.

Royal Commission on the Economic State and Prospects of Newfoundland and Labrador. *Report*. St. John's: Queen's Printer, 1967.

Royal Commission on the Economic Union and Development Prospects for Canada. *Report,* 3 Vols. Ottawa: 1985.

——. *Submission of the Government of Newfoundland and Labrador*. St. John's: Queen's Printer, 1983.

Royal Commission on Education, Public Services and Provincial-Municipal Relations. Nova Scotia. *Report*. 1974.

Royal Commission on Employment and Unemployment. Newfoundland. *Work and Unemployment in St. John's*. 1986.

Royal Commission on Employment and Unemployment, Newfoundland and Labrador. *Perspectives on the Newfoundland Labour Market. Background Report*. St. John's: Queen's Printer, 1986.

Royal Commission on Financial Arrangements between the Dominion and the Maritime Provinces. *Report*. 1935.

Royal Commission on Maritime Claims. *Report*. 1926.

Royal Commission on Taxation and Revenue Structure of the City of St. John's. Newfoundland. *Report*. 1966.

Rumney, Thomas. *The Urban Geography of Canada: A Selected Bibliography*. Monticello, Illinois: Vance Bibliographies, 1988.

Sacouman, R.J. "Atlantic Canada." *The New Practical Guide to Canadian Political Economy,* D. Drache and W. Clement (eds.). Toronto: Lorimer, 1985.

——. "The 'Peripheral' Maritimes and Canada-Wide Marxist Political Economy." *Studies in Political Economy* 6 (Autumn 1981): 135–50.

——. "Regional Uneven Development, Regionalism and Struggle." *Introduction to Sociology, an Alternate Approach*. Toronto: Gage, 1983.

——. "Semi-Proletarianization and Rural Underdevelopment in the Maritimes." *Canadian Review of Anthropology and Sociology* 17 (1980): 232–45.

Sager, Eric. "Dependency, Underdevelopment, and the Economic History of the Atlantic Provinces." *Acadiensis* XVII, 1 (Autumn 1987): 117–37.

——. "The Port of St. John's Newfoundland, 1840–1889: A Preliminary Analysis." *Ships and Shipbuilding in the North Atlantic Region,* K. Matthews and G. Panting (eds.). St. John's: Memorial University, 1978.

Sager, Eric and Gerald Panting. *Maritime Capital: The Shipping Industry in Atlantic Canada, 1820–1914*. Montreal: McGill-Queen's University Press, 1990.

Sampson, Gordon H. *North Bar Remembered: North Sydney's Centennial and Bicentennial*. North Sydney, N.S.: 1985.

Sandberg, L. Anders. "Dependent Development, Labour and the Trenton Steel Works, Nova Scotia, c. 1900–1943." *Labour/Le Travail* 27 (Spring 1991): 127–62.

Saunders, S.A. *The Economic History of the Maritime Provinces*. A study prepared for the Royal Commission on Dominion-Provincial Relations. Ottawa: King's Printer, 1939.

——. *Studies in the Economy of the Maritime Provinces*. Toronto: Macmillan, 1939.

Savoie, Donald. *Federal-Provincial Collaboration: The Canada-New Brunswick General Development Agreement*. Montreal: McGill-Queens University Press, 1981.

——. *Le lutte pour le développement: Le cas du Nord-Est.* Québec: Université de Québec Press, 1989.

——. *Regional Economic Development: Canada's Search For Solutions.* Toronto, University of Toronto Press, 1986 (second edition, 1992).

Seager, Allen. "Minto, New Brunswick: A Study in Class Relations Between the Wars." *Labour/Le Travail* 5 (Spring 1980): 81–132.

Sears, Garry Martin. *Canadian Manufacturing and Urban Growth.* Ottawa: Carleton University Press, 1976.

Senate Committee on Agriculture. *Kent County Can Be Saved.* Ottawa: Queen's Printer, 1976.

Shand, G.V. "Windsor: A Centre of Shipbuilding." *Nova Scotia Historical Society Collections.* 1970.

Sharpe, Christopher A. *Heritage Conservation and Development Control in a Speculative Environment: The Case of St. John's.* 1986.

Sharpe, Errol. *A People's History of Prince Edward Island.* Toronto: Steel Rail Publishing, 1976.

Sheppard, Burt and Associates. *St. John's Heritage Conservation Area Study.* St. John's: 1976.

Sherwood, Roland H. "The Great Campbellton Fire." *The Maritime Advocate and Busy East.* February, 1947.

Sider, Gerald M. *Culture and Class in Anthropology and History: A Newfoundland Illustration.* Cambridge: Cambridge University Press, 1986,

Simmons, James. *Canada as an Urban System: A Conceptual Framework.* Toronto: Centre for Urban and Community Studies, University of Toronto, 1974.

——. *The Growth of the Canadian Urban System.* Toronto: Centre for Urban and Community Studies, University of Toronto, 1974.

——. *Recent Trends and Patterns in Canadian Settlement, 1976–1981.* Toronto: Centre for Urban and Community Studies, University of Toronto, 1984.

Sinclair, A.M. *The Economic Base of the Halifax Metropolitan Area and Some Implications of Recent Population Forecasts.* Halifax: Dalhousie University, Institute of Public Affairs, 1961.

Sinclair, Peter R. "Fishermen of Northwest Newfoundland." *Journal of Canadian Studies* 19, 1 (1984): 34–47.

——. "From Peasants to Corporations: The Development of Capitalist Agriculture in Canada's Maritime Provinces." *Contradictions in Canadian Society,* J.A. Fry (ed.). Toronto: John Wiley and Sons, 1984.

——. *From Traps to Draggers: Domestic Commodity Production in Northwest Newfoundland, 1850–1982.* St. John's: Institute for Social and Economic Research, 1985.

Sitwell, O.F.G. "Land Use and Settlement Patterns in Pictou County, Nova Scotia." Ph.D. Thesis, University of Toronto, 1968.

Skolnik, M.L. (ed.). *Viewpoints on Communities in Crisis.* St. John's: Institute for Social and Economic Research, 1968.

Smallwood, J.R. *The New Newfoundland.* New York: Macmillan and Co., 1931.

Smith, David Charles. *Changing Values: The Human Impact of Urbanization.* Scarborough, Ont.: Bellhaven House, 1971.

Smitheram, V., D. Milne and S. Dasgupta (eds.). *The Garden Transformed: Prince Edward Island 1945–1980.* Charlottetown: Ragweed Press, 1982.

Some Economic and Social Characteristics of Kent County, Province of New Brunswick. Fredericton: Office of the Economic Advisor, Government of New Brunswick, 1968.

Speller, R.G. "The Halifax Metropolitan Area, 1947." *Reorganization of Provincial-Municipal Relations in Nova Scotia*. Halifax: Nova Scotia Department of Municipal Affairs, 1949.

Spence-Sales, Harold. *Moncton Renewed: Urban Renewal Survey*. City of Moncton: 1958.

Squires, W. Austin. *History of Fredericton: The Last 200 Years*. Fredericton: City of Fredericton, 1980.

Stanley, Della M.M. *Louis Robichaud: A Decade of Power*. Halifax: Nimbus Publishing, 1984.

Staveley, Michael. "Newfoundland: Economy and Society at the Margin." *Heartland and Hinterland: A Geography of Canada*, L.D. McCann (ed.). Toronto: 1987.

Stelter, G.A. (ed.). *Cities and Urbanization: Canadian Historical Perspectives*. Toronto: Copp Clark Pitman, 1990.

Stelter, G.A. *Approaches to the Study of Urban Settlement: History, Planning, Geography*. Waterloo, Ont.: Faculty of Environmental Studies, University of Waterloo, 1974.

Stelter, Gilbert. "A Regional Framework for Urban History." *Urban History Review* XII, 3 (February 1985): 193–205.

Stelter, G.A. and A.F.J. Artibise. *Canada's Urban Past: A Bibliography to 1980 and Guide to Canadian Urban Studies*. Vancouver: University of British Columbia Press, 1981.

Stelter, G.A. and A.F.J. Artibise (eds.). *The Canadian City: Essays in Urban and Social History*. Ottawa: Carleton University Press, 1984.

——. *Shaping the Urban Landscape: Aspects of the Canadian City-Building Process*. Ottawa: Carleton University Press, 1982.

Stephenson, Gordon. *A Redevelopment Study of Halifax, Nova Scotia*. Halifax: City of Halifax, 1957.

Stewart, Bryce Morrison. *Sydney, Nova Scotia: the report of a brief investigation of social conditions in the city which indicate the need of an intensive social survey, the lines of which are herein suggested, made by the Board of Temperance and Moral Reform of Social Service and Evangelism of the Presbyterian Church*. Toronto: 1913.

Stone, Leroy O. *Urban Development in Canada: An Introduction to the Demographic Aspects*. Ottawa: Dominion Bureau of Statistics, 1967.

Sutherland, D.A. "Halifax Merchants and the pursuit of Development, 1783–1850." *Canadian Historical Review* LIX, 1 (March 1978): 1–17.

——. "Halifax 1815–1914: 'Colony to Colony'." *Urban History Review* No. 1 (1975): 7–11.

Taylor, John H. "Urban Autonomy in Canada: Its Evolution and Decline." *Power and Place: Canadian Urban Development in the North American Context*. Gilbert A. Stelter and Alan F.J. Artibise (eds.). Vancouver: 1986.

Tennyson, Brian. "Economic Nationalism and Confederation: A Case Study of Cape Breton." *Acadiensis* II, 1 (Autumn 1976): 39–53.

Thornton, Patricia. "The Problem of Out-Migration from Atlantic Canada, 1871–1921: A New Look." *Acadiensis* XV, 1 (Autumn 1985): 3–34.

Traves, Tom. *The State and Enterprise: Canadian Manufacturers and the Federal Government 1971–1931*. Toronto: University of Toronto Press, 1979.

Trudeau, P.E. "The Expansion of the Atlantic Economy." *Atlantic Advocate* 59, 7 (March 1969): 12–16.

Truro Centennial Committee. *Town of Truro Centennial, 1875–1975, Marking 100 years as an Incorporated Community.* Truro, 1975.

Tuck, Robert C. "Georgetown: The Town that Time Forgot." *The Island Magazine* (1978).

Tupper, Alan. "Public Enterprise as Social Welfare: The Case of the Cape Breton Development Corporation." *Canadian Public Policy* 4, 4 (Autumn 1978): 530–46.

Tye, Dianne. "The Housing of A Workforce: Workers' Housing in Amherst, N.S., 1900–1914." *Society for the Study of Architecture in Canada Bulletin* XI, 3 (September 1986): 14–16.

Urban Population Growth and Municipal Organization. Kingston, Ont.: Institute of Local Government, Queen's University. 1973.

Vaison, R. and P.C. Aucoin. "Municipal Politics in Canada: Class and Voting in the 1968 Halifax Mayoralty Election." *University of Windsor Review* 5, 2 (Spring 1970): 68–78.

Veltmeyer, Henry. "The Underdevelopment of Atlantic Canada." *Review of Radical Political Economics* 10, 3 (Fall 1978): 95–105.

Wallace, C.M. "Saint John Boosters and the Railroads in the Mid-Nineteenth Century." *Acadiensis* VI, 1 (Autumn 1976): 71–91.

——. "Saint John, N.B." *Urban History Review* 1 (1975): 12–21.

Weaver, John C. *Shaping the Canadian City: Essays on Urban Politics and Policy, 1890–1920.* Toronto: Institute of Public Administration of Canada, 1977.

——. "Reconstruction of the Richmond District of Halifax: A Canadian Episode in Public Housing and Town Planning, 1918–1921." *Plan Canada* 16, 1 (March 1976): 36–47.

Whelan, Hugh. "Public Policy and Regional Development: The Experience of the Atlantic Provinces." *The Prospects of Change: Proposals for Canada's Future,* A. Rotstein (ed.). Toronto: McGraw-Hill, 1965.

Weir, Gail. *The Miners of Wabana: Story of the Iron Ore Miners of Bell Island.* St. John's: 1989.

Williams, R. "Inshore Fishermen, Unionization, and the Struggle against Underdevelopment Today." *Underdevelopment and Social Movements in Atlantic Canada,* R.J. Brym and R.J. Sacouman (eds.). Toronto: New Hogtown Press, 1979.

Winson, Anthony. "The uneven development of Canadian agriculture: Farming in the Maritimes and Ontario." *Canadian Journal of Sociology* 10, 4 (1985): 411–38.

Winter, J.R. (ed.). *The Atlantic Provinces in Canada: Where Do We Go From Here? Conference.* Halifax: Atlantic Provinces Economic Council, 1981.

Woodfine, William. "Canada's Atlantic Provinces: A Study in Regional Economic Retardation." *Economics Canada,* Mel Watkins and D.F. Foster (eds.). Toronto: McGraw-Hill, 1964.

Wylie, Peter J. "When Markets Fail: Electrification and Maritime Industrial Decline in the 1920s." *Acadiensis* XXVII, 1 (Autumn 1987): 74–96.

Wynn, Graeme. "Ethnic Migrations and Atlantic Canada: Geographical Perspectives." *Canadian Ethnic Studies* 18, 1 (1986).

——. "The Maritimes: The Geography of Fragmentation and Underdevelopment." *Heartland and Hinterland: A Geography of Canada,* L.D. McCann (ed.). Toronto: 1987.

——. *Timber Colony: A Historical Geography of Early Nineteenth Century New Brunswick.* Toronto: 1981.

Young, R.A. "'And the People Will Sink into Despair': Reconstruction in New
  Brunswick, 1942–52." *Canadian Historical Review* LXIX (June 1988):
  127–66.
Zwicker, F. Homer. *Royal Commission Reports and Related Action.* Halifax: The
  Institute of Public Affairs, Dalhousie University, 1960.

Contributors

Tom Archibald, a native of Bridgewater and a graduate of Carleton University's School of Journalism with a major in History, is studying Law at Osgoode Hall.

Angus Bickerton, though a native of Manotick, has roots deep in the Maritimes. A graduate of McGill University's history program, he is currently studying Law at the University of Alberta.

David Boucher is from Vermont and has completed a masters degree in Canadian Studies at Carleton University. His thesis topic was *Metropolitan Growth in Atlantic Canada: Saint John and the Throughway*. He is proceeding to doctoral work in urban studies at the University of Wisconsin.

Peter Brander is a native of Dalhousie working as a legislative assistant in the House of Commons. His program was in Carleton University's Institute of Political Economy, where his thesis was *The Political Economy of Community Development, Dalhousie, N.B., 1860–1990*.

Stephen Burridge, a native of Fredericton, has degrees from both Acadia University and University of New Brunswick, as well as his M.A. from Carleton University in History, where his thesis topic was *The Busy East: Boosting the Maritimes, 1910–1925*.

Eleanor Glenn is an Ottawa teacher and is graduate of the honours program in Women's Studies. Her interest in historical drama leads to readings and performances relating to Ottawa Valley history to various community groups.

Tomoko Hagiwara, a native of Japan is completing a masters degree in Canadian Studies at Carleton University. Her interest in children's literature in Canada is combined with an active career as a guide for visiting Japanese businessmen and scholars alike.

Bruce Lauer, with the Department of Health and Welfare, has had an active career in Nova Scotia. He is completing a masters degree in the history of food and drug regulation.

Del Muise, teaches Canadian and Atlantic Provinces History at Carleton University.

Donna Sacuta is a British Columbia native with an insatiable interest in Nova Scotia's labour and working class history. She has completed an honours degree in Labour Studies at Carleton University.

Tim Simpson, a graduate of Carleton University's honours history program, has completed teacher training in Syracuse, N.Y.

Index

Acadia University, 58
Acadians, 18, 65–67
Africville, 79, 80, 103
Amherst, 11, 20, 29–31, 35, 37, 75, 89–92
Anglo-Newfoundland Development Company, 99
Annapolis Valley, 12, 29, 58
Antigonish, 60, 63
Atlantic Canada Opportunities Agency (ACOA), 47
Atlantic Development Board, 45
Atlantic Provinces Economic Council, 44, 45
Avalon Peninsula, 22, 69, 75, 86

Bathurst 17, 65, 66, 68
Bedford, 76
Bedford Basin, 19, 44, 79
Bell Island, 22, 97, 98
Belledune, 67, 69
BESCO (British Empire Steel Corporation), 94
Bishop's Falls, 99
Bluenose, 61

Campbellton, 17, 65, 66
Canadian National Railway, 16, 37
Canadian Pacific Railway, 29, 82
Canso, 60
Canso Causeway, 44
Cape Breton, 2, 4, 13, 18–20, 22, 32, 35, 44, 46, 48, 58, 60, 61, 63, 88, 90, 92–97, 100
Cape Breton Development Corporation (DEVCO), 95
Careless, J.M.S., 25–26
Centralization Program (Newfoundland) 69
Charlottetown, 11, 13, 21, 27, 45, 46, 57, 58, 103, 104
Chatham, 17, 65
Coal, 11, 19, 20, 22, 26, 32, 34, 35, 37, 38, 46, 48, 60, 61, 67, 88–90, 92–97, 100, 104

Confederation, 9, 13, 23, 25, 27, 28, 32, 35, 37–39, 46, 48, 58, 66, 77, 82, 102
Corner Brook, 11, 12, 22, 75, 98–100
Cumberland Hotel, 29

Dalhousie, 17, 65, 66, 92
Davidson, E.D., Company, 61
Dartmouth, 19, 44, 75–78, 80
Department of Regional Economic Expansion (DREE), 45, 47, 68
Department of Regional Industrial Expansion, 47
Depression, 25, 36–38, 61
Diefenbaker, John G., 43
Dieppe, 91
Digby, 5, 33, 60, 62
Digby waterfront, 33
Dominion Steel and Coal Company, 32

Eaton, T., Company 16
Edmundston, 17, 56, 57
Equal Opportunity Program (New Brunswick), 46
European and North American Railway, 90

Fort Needam Park, 39
Fortune, 32
Fredericton, 11, 13, 16, 17, 27, 32, 35, 37, 42, 47, 48, 54, 55, 58, 59, 93, 96, 103
Fund for Rural Economic Development (FRED), 45, 67

Glace Bay, 34, 48, 92, 93, 95, 97, 104
Goldenberg Commission, 84
Grand Falls, 11, 12, 22, 75, 99, 100
Greenwood, 40, 58
Gulf Oil Refinery (Port Hawkesbury), 43

Halifax, 11, 18–20, 24, 25, 27–29, 34, 35, 39, 40, 42, 43–47, 58, 63, 75–85, 87, 88, 103
Halifax and Dartmouth Metropolitan Authority, 77
Halifax waterfront, 80

Hartland, 56
Heavy water plant, 44, 48, 95
Hillsborough River, 57
Historic Properties, 46, 104
Howe, C.D., 40
Hydrostone (Halifax), 79

Innis, H.A., 25
Intercolonial Railway, 16, 28, 30, 66, 89,
    90, 92
International Paper Company, 66
Inverness, 60–61
Irving, K.C., 83

Kentville, 58

Labrador, 12, 22, 23, 39, 69, 97, 100
Lancaster, 82, 84
Liverpool, 61
Lunenburg 19, 60–62, 71, 72, 77

Mabou Coal Mines, 61
Market Slip (Saint John), 82
Marysville, 40, 54, 55
McCain, 49, 56, 72
McCann, L.D., 25, 26, 32, 37, 77, 80, 94,
    96
Michelin tire plant, 20, 64, 72, 96, 97
Milltown, 40, 54
Miramichi River, 17, 65, 66
Moncton, 11, 12, 16, 28, 34, 36, 37, 47, 75,
    88–92, 103, 104
Mount Pearl, 87

National Housing Act, 42
National Policy, 28, 31–34, 54, 73, 88, 89,
    96, 103
New Glasgow, 11, 20, 32, 75, 96, 97
New Waterford, 92, 95
Newcastle, 17, 65, 66
Newfoundland Railroad, 29, 86, 98
Newfoundland Resettlement Program, 69
North Sydney, 92

Oromocto, 17, 40, 55

Pictou County, 11, 31, 37, 40, 88, 89, 94,
    96, 97, 100
Port Hawkesbury, 43, 44, 60, 63, 64
Provincial Development Plan (Prince
    Edward Island), 45
Pulp and paper industry, 12, 17, 22, 37,
    56, 57, 61, 65, 66, 88, 96, 98, 100, 102

Quispamis, 84

Riverview, 12, 90, 91
Robichaud, Louis, 47, 69
Rothesay, 84
Royal Commission on Canada's Economic
    Prospects, 42

Sackville, 19, 76, 91
Saint Francis Xavier University, 60
Saint John, 11, 12, 15–17, 27, 29, 33, 34,
    40, 44, 46, 52–57, 59, 71, 75, 80,
    82–85, 87, 88, 90, 103, 104
Saint John Drydock Company, 83
Saint John waterfront, 83
Scotia Square (Halifax), 77
Scotia Steel, 89
Senator's Corner (Glace Bay), 93
Shediac, 90, 91
Shelburne, 60, 62
Shingle Mill, 27
Smallwood, J.R., 69
Springhill, 20, 32, 92, 104
St. George, 57
St. John's, 22, 26, 29, 39, 42, 44, 69, 75, 85
Stellarton, 97, 104
Stephenson Report, 79
STORA (Forest Industries Ltd.), 63, 64
Summerside, 21, 40
Sussex, 55
Sydney, 11, 19, 31, 32, 34, 37, 40, 48, 75,
    88, 89, 92–96, 103
Sydney Mines, 32, 34, 89, 92, 94, 95
Sydney Steel (SYSCO), 95, 96

The Throughway (Saint John), 84, 85
Trans-Canada Highway, 42, 91
Trenton, 26, 35, 40, 94, 96, 97
Trudeau Pierre E., 45
Truro, 13, 19, 20, 40, 58, 77

University of New Brunswick, 36, 44, 55,
    59, 61

Wabana, 22, 97, 98
Westville, 97
Windsor, 13, 19, 40, 58, 77, 99
Wolfville, 58
World War I, 16, 17, 22, 25, 28, 31, 34, 35,
    41, 92, 94, 97,, 103
World War II, 12–14, 21, 23, 39, 54, 60,
    78, 80, 83, 84, 90, 92, 100

Yarmouth, 11, 20, 29, 40, 60, 62, 63